NA2750.S24 1979
420479

NA
2750
.S24
1979

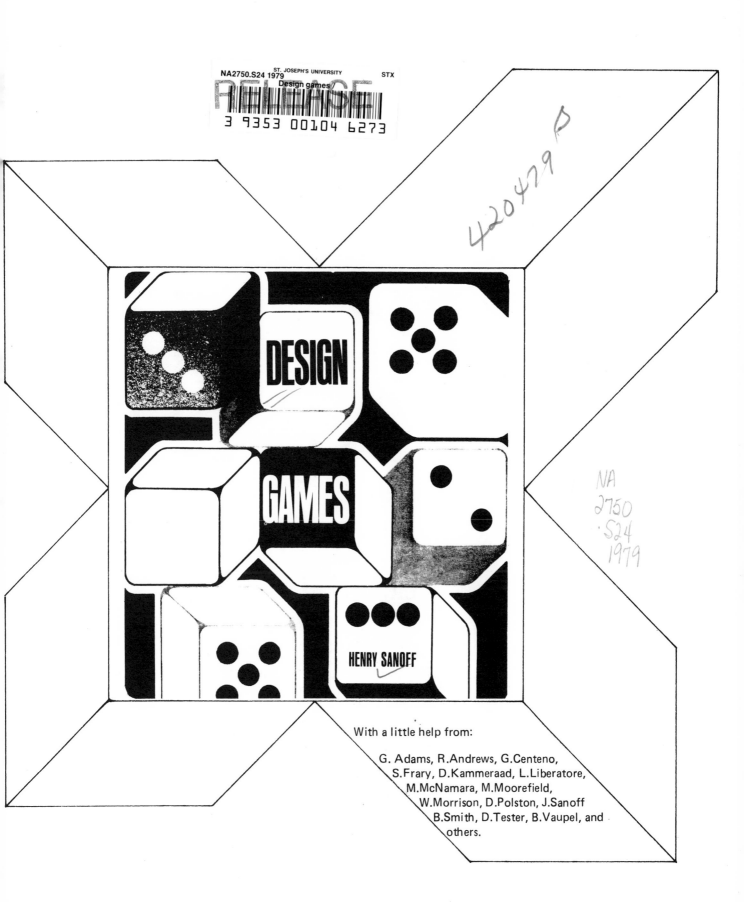

With a little help from:

G. Adams, R.Andrews, G.Centeno,
S.Frary, D.Kammeraad, L.Liberatore,
M.McNamara, M.Moorefield,
W.Morrison, D.Polston, J.Sanoff
B.Smith, D.Tester, B.Vaupel, and
others.

193117

Library of Congress Cataloging in Publication Data

Sanoff, Henry.
    Design games.

    1. Architectural design--Study and teaching--
Simulation methods. 2. Simulation games in
education. I. Title.
NA2750.S24   309.2'12   79-10792
ISBN 0-913232-63-7

Experimental Edition

To readers—owners of this book: please feel free to cut, fold or mutilate the pages. Above all, try to use our materials as a guide to what you might do.

All the games in the book contain three basic ingredients: rules of the game, concepts (or pictures depicting concepts) and recording methods. You may substitute your own pictures to use with our rules or you can use our pictures and substitute your rules for ours.

Environmental games provide a way to engage people in discussions designed to help them to discover their personal differences while the discussion focuses on a particular set of concepts. We especially like this approach for workshops with teachers, architects or students because it provides all the participants with a hands-on opportunity to explore environmental issues. We believe that learning occurs best when theory and experience are connected activities. Thus, the games contain the theoretical concepts and you, the participant, are involved in an exploratory-discovery process that provides the experience. This experience, however, is only a catalyst for others that you can provide, since the game experience is a simulation, an abstraction of a real event. For learning to occur you, the student, should relate personal experiences to a particular place and discover your unique relationships.

CONTENTS

WHY DESIGN GAMES? **1**

1 DESIGNING GAMES **3**

2 EVOCATIVE GAMES **9**

Wish Poem **10**
Spaces that Connect **12**
Environmental Education **14**
Descriptive Words **18**

3 GAMES ABOUT DESIGN CHOICES **21**

Issues Auction **22**
Best Fit Slide Rule **24**
Design Ballot **32**
Household Activities **36**
Plan Alternatives **38**
House Image **40**
Site Alternatives **42**
House Choice **44**
Strategies for Improving Downtown Environments **46**

4 GAMES ABOUT CONSENSUS DECISIONS **51**

Planning Outdoor Play **53**
Playground Equipment Planning **58**
Learning Environments for Children **68**
Senior Center Design **75**
Relating Objectives for Learning to Education **76**
The Challenge of the Environment **80**
Role Play **84**
Knowledge of Emerging Environmental Preservation Strategies **89**

5 EVALUATING GAME SESSIONS **93**

Questionnaire **95**
References **99**

WHY DESIGN GAMES

Gaming is an approach to problem solving that engages a real life situation compressed in time so that the essential characteristics of the problem are open to examination. This technique is particularly appealing for designers because it permits learning about the process of change in a dynamic environment requiring periodic decisions. Essentially we are identifying a complex problem and abstracting its essence, a process referred to as simulation. A game, then, is a particular type of simulation. Mathematicians and scientists also use simulation methods to understand their world, and they frequently use mathematical formulae or symbols to communicate and model their areas of investigation.

Designers are individuals concerned with creating environments that are congruent with the needs and life styles of the using populations. The past decade has witnessed the growth of knowledge about user needs, preferences and behavior. These data were generated from studies that often represent a moment in the life space of a particular environment. While this rapidly growing reservoir of information has substantively contributed to the development of the design professions, other methods for understanding user needs and values are equally important to capture the dynamic aspects of the environment. Games represent one method.

Our games have been developed to facilitate an understanding of strategies for solving problems and imparting information in a meaningful way. While games help to understand the complex interweaving of environmental, social and technological forces, they can also be used to provide insights into situations so familiar that their characteristics are not perceived. Games help sharpen perceptions.

1

One particular feature of games that we are all familiar with is winning and losing. We advocate group discussions that are collaborative in nature and that require consensus decisions. We believe this is important because--as issues become more complex and interconnected--solutions must be generated which will satisfy the affected population. Bargaining and voting methods create situations which have only two sides. These methods are increasingly more unrealistic and usually force people to take extreme positions in order to influence votes. Also, losers in any situation are usually disgruntled. Therefore, the decision-making techniques utilized in this book are primarily based on collaborative planning.

All of the techniques included here have gone through the test of experience. In fact, this collection is an off-the-shelf assemblage of materials that have been in use for the past five years. Each method was developed to accomplish specific tasks ranging from increasing people's awareness to particular environmental issues, to teaching concepts and relationships, to clarifying value differences between decision makers. The primary thrust of all methods is towards the identification of issues bearing on improving the quality of the environment.

Design Games is a practical guide describing techniques for effectively involving user groups, design professionals, planners, students and citizens concerned about the quality of the environment, in design decisions. The games can help people grasp complex relationships about the environment in order to create changes that are responsive to human needs.

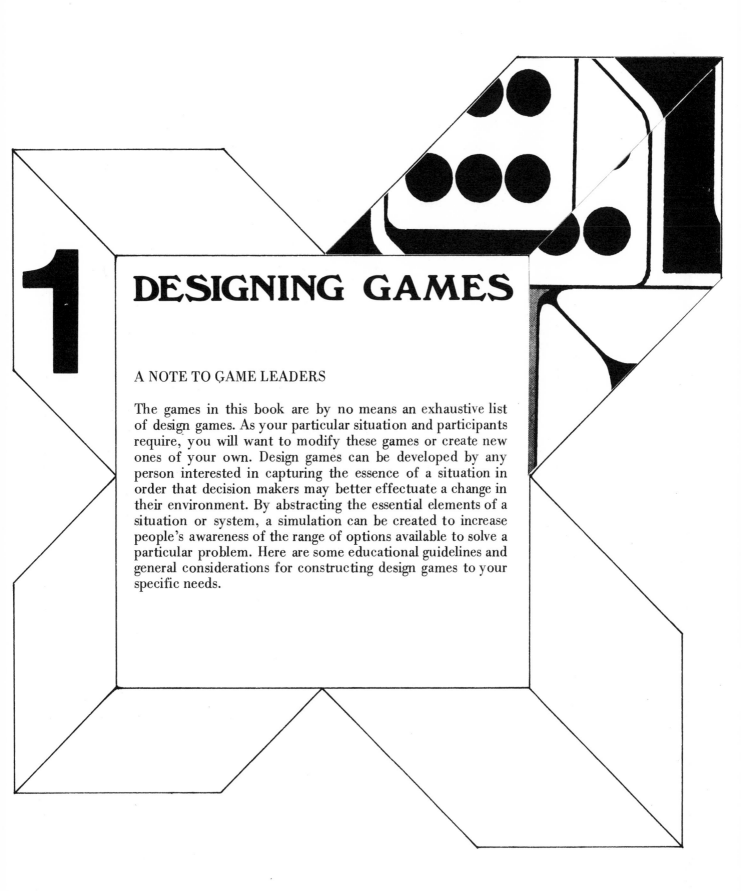

DESIGNING GAMES

A NOTE TO GAME LEADERS

The games in this book are by no means an exhaustive list of design games. As your particular situation and participants require, you will want to modify these games or create new ones of your own. Design games can be developed by any person interested in capturing the essence of a situation in order that decision makers may better effectuate a change in their environment. By abstracting the essential elements of a situation or system, a simulation can be created to increase people's awareness of the range of options available to solve a particular problem. Here are some educational guidelines and general considerations for constructing design games to your specific needs.

RULES OF THE GAME

VALUES

Values are those beliefs we hold to have some intrinsic personal worth. Personal values include feelings and attitudes that characterize and influence our behavior. Value differences between individuals often account for an inability to achieve agreement in group problem solving situations. Quite often so-called "differences of opinions" are rooted in basic value differences that are not made explicit. The ability to achieve personal control as well as group effectiveness lies in one's ability to clarify personal beliefs about the situation under examination. Values clarification methods encourage people to examine their own beliefs in a manner similar to those where scientific methods aid the scientists' exploration. This approach permits the study of patterns and choices about one's self. Each game compels the participants to make decisions between alternatives. In making the choices, individuals have to examine their feelings, self concepts and values. Since participants respond to a design situation with different values and beliefs, incorporate in your game design the opportunity for participants to share those differences. It is the first step in the process of consensus decision making.

STRUCTURE

Games emphasize learning through direct experience. An important ingredient in this alternative method of learning is the need for structure, particularly for the group experience. "Structure" is merely a label for those activities that focus the group process, control extraneous variables, and increase the probability that certain learning will occur for the participants. Although the learning goals of the structured experience can be specified and the outcomes are somewhat predictable, the structured experience does not dictate what a participant should learn. Its intent is to facilitate learning that would otherwise be haphazard and diffuse. The structured experience is a function of the objectives of the experience, the content and the techniques employed to focus learning. The game techniques employed to direct learning include activities such as making or building something, discussions, summarizations, board games, interviews, inventories or check lists, role playing and tasks.

INDIVIDUAL OBJECTIVES

The individual objectives or learning goals of a structured experience may include cognitive, affective and skill-building aspects. The cognitive goals may include increasing awareness of the factual content, the incorporation and use of the content, generalization from the particular, and conceptual organization. Building the participant's self-awareness, insight and empathy are some of the affective aspects of learning objectives. The development and implementation of skills such as listening and problem solving are some of the skill building objectives.

GROUP OBJECTIVES

Each game in this book structures the players' experiences about some aspect of interpersonal group behavior. The types of experiences outlined below are the behavioral basis for designing games.

Interpersonal Communication:	The successful functioning in groups depends upon the development of trust, learning how to listen and develop various types of relationships.
Group Problem Solving:	The ability of groups to engage in a situation requiring their ability to resolve a conflict and to provide a solution through consensus.
Organizational Development:	The ability of participants to organize themselves into work groups for production and planning as well as team building.
Awareness Expansion:	The development of sensory awareness is linked to broadening the individual's self-perception and enlarging personal boundaries.
Personal Feedback:	When participants interact, there is a giving and receiving of information through informal as well as formal means.
Consensus Cooperation:	Cooperative strategies are necessary for participants to experience "winning".

SCENARIO

Another important aspect of games is their "scenario"—the conception of what situation is going to be represented. The game's objectives should serve as a primary factor in the design of a scenario, but there are four general considerations entering into the scenario composition: the time setting, the environmental setting, the level of detail, and the level of knowledge and characteristics of the game participants.

The time setting is an important factor in that the players should not be confronted with events projected so far into the future that current strategies and policy implications are constrained by uncertainty. Environmental settings are necessary to establish the parameters or boundaries examined by the game. For designers, this becomes the essential ingredient that characterizes features of the physical environment. The third consideration arises out of the natural limitation of the players in the amount of detail they can absorb and manipulate. Finally, the participants should be considered in determining the degree of thoroughness of the scenario. The level of detail necessary for high school students would be different than that required for professionals who bring with them particular skills.

Credibility and consistency are the key qualities necessary for a successful scenario.

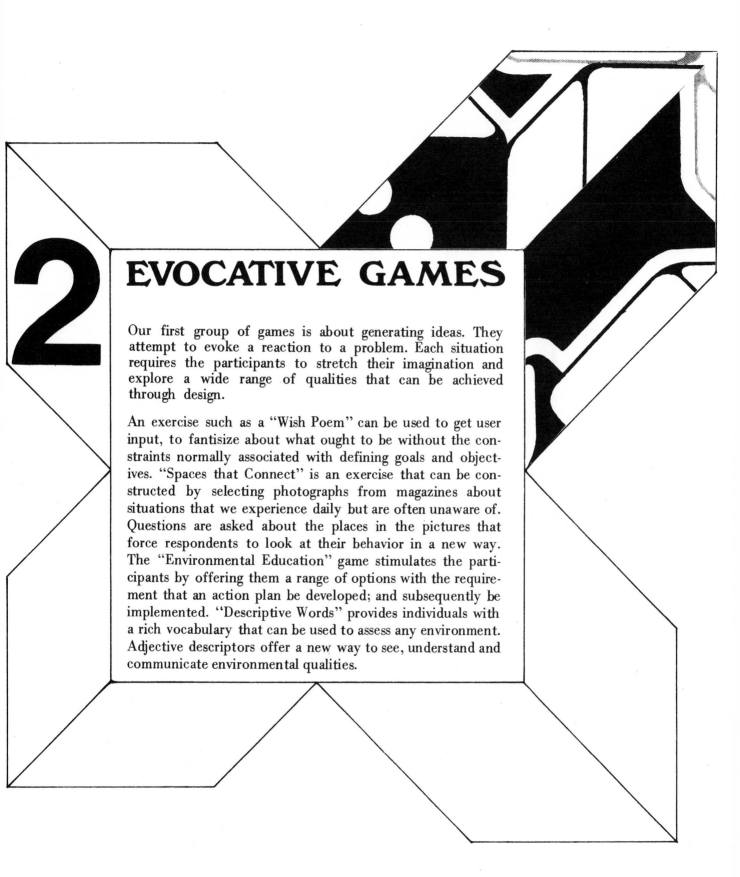

2 EVOCATIVE GAMES

Our first group of games is about generating ideas. They attempt to evoke a reaction to a problem. Each situation requires the participants to stretch their imagination and explore a wide range of qualities that can be achieved through design.

An exercise such as a "Wish Poem" can be used to get user input, to fantisize about what ought to be without the constraints normally associated with defining goals and objectives. "Spaces that Connect" is an exercise that can be constructed by selecting photographs from magazines about situations that we experience daily but are often unaware of. Questions are asked about the places in the pictures that force respondents to look at their behavior in a new way. The "Environmental Education" game stimulates the participants by offering them a range of options with the requirement that an action plan be developed; and subsequently be implemented. "Descriptive Words" provides individuals with a rich vocabulary that can be used to assess any environment. Adjective descriptors offer a new way to see, understand and communicate environmental qualities.

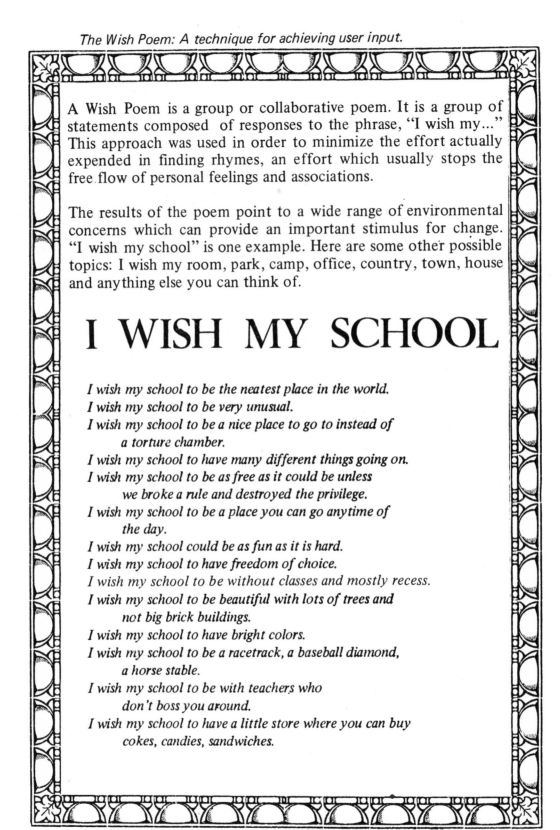

A Wish Poem is a group or collaborative poem. It is a group of statements composed of responses to the phrase, "I wish my..." This approach was used in order to minimize the effort actually expended in finding rhymes, an effort which usually stops the free flow of personal feelings and associations.

The results of the poem point to a wide range of environmental concerns which can provide an important stimulus for change. "I wish my school" is one example. Here are some other possible topics: I wish my room, park, camp, office, country, town, house and anything else you can think of.

I WISH MY SCHOOL

I wish my school to be the neatest place in the world.
I wish my school to be very unusual.
I wish my school to be a nice place to go to instead of
*   a torture chamber.*
I wish my school to have many different things going on.
I wish my school to be as free as it could be unless
*   we broke a rule and destroyed the privilege.*
I wish my school to be a place you can go anytime of
*   the day.*
I wish my school could be as fun as it is hard.
I wish my school to have freedom of choice.
I wish my school to be without classes and mostly recess.
I wish my school to be beautiful with lots of trees and
*   not big brick buildings.*
I wish my school to have bright colors.
I wish my school to be a racetrack, a baseball diamond,
*   a horse stable.*
I wish my school to be with teachers who
*   don't boss you around.*
I wish my school to have a little store where you can buy
*   cokes, candies, sandwiches.*

from Henry Sanoff, *Seeing the Environment: An Advocacy Approach,* (Learning Environments, 1973)

from American Institute of Architects, *Built Environment Guidebook: How to Conduct Environmental Education Workshops for Teachers and Architects,* (Washington, D.C., 1977)

See pages 98–101 for enlarged versions of these photos of connecting spaces.

A
SPACES
THAT CONNECT

A psychologist friend of ours, Robert Sommer, made an interesting observation; he noted that the built environment "affects most people just beyond the focus of their awareness." Here is a game that can help to sensitize people about an important element of our built environment, spaces that connect.

Each day we spend time going from one place to another. And, whether it is during school time, for business or for pleasure, we tend to be more aware of the places we are going to than the places we use to get there.

Our daily walking behavior takes us through a wide variety of indoor and outdoor passages. We decide upon the appropriateness of a particular route from the cues or subtle bits of information embedded in the path features. Whether we are hurried or desire to take a leisurely walk we look for those features, such as ground cover, amount of enclosure, path width, traffic and visual variety to aid us in making the best decision.

The route we choose to a destination is often influenced by the purpose of the trip. We are all familiar with the famous 'short-cut' or the shortest route to a particular destination. The short-cut is a way to reduce the time to reach a destination, particularly if we are late. Often it permits the time saved to be budgeted for other activities. Each selection we make is based on the particular features of the route or how interesting it appears to be.

There are three typical situations that we frequently encounter in our walking behavior. They are destination oriented but rushed, destination oriented but leisurely and exploratory, or leisurely with no particular designation in mind. For each walking situation there might be an appropriate route. Let's use the set of pictures to select different walking routes.

	Situations	Groups	Qualities of the spaces which influence your decision.
1	**Destination Oriented, and Rushed.** "Yipes, I've got only five minutes to get there."		
2	**Destination Oriented, but Leisurely.** "I've got to get there by nine and its only seven-thirty."		
3	**Exploratory, and Leisurely.** "I've got some extra time, why not find some interesting places along this route."		

B
SORT FOR SIMILARITIES

Look through the pictures and group them according to the similarities you find in them. Record the letters within each set of pictures in the box titled GROUPS. Then, examine all the pictures in each group and record why you think they are similar, in the appropriate box.

Groups	How they are similar

C
DESIGN YOUR OWN ROUTE

From the origins and destinations listed below, sort through the set of pictures to find the connector spaces you would prefer to use for each situation. For each pair of locations select at least three connecting spaces.

Home	_____	**School**
Classroom	_____	**Cafeteria**
Home	_____	**Best friend's house**
Terminal entrance	_____	**Entering airplane**
Parking lot	_____	**Dentists' office**

A GAME TO HELP GENERATE IDEAS FOR ENVIRONMENTAL PROJECTS

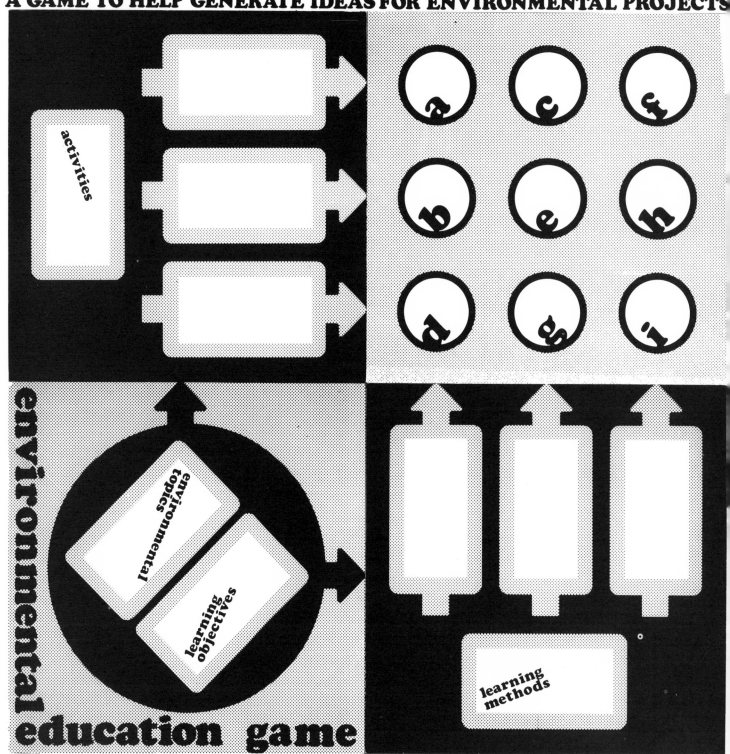

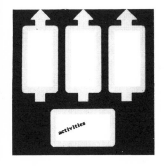
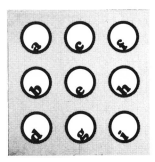
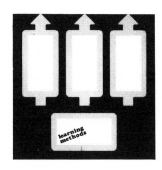

Find out how furniture arrangements can effect the way a space is used

Find out how to collect and organize information for design decisions

Examine how color effects our feelings

Find out why energy resources are problems for designers

Compare people circulation with vehicular circulation

Examine the purpose and use of parks in the city

Examine what architects do

Discover how your personal activities relate to each other

Compare colors in the built environment with those in nature

Examine how spatial use has suggested the shape of spaces

Examine the role of participants in the design process

Discover how certain places influence interaction between people

Examine how the human dimension effects design

Examine how places built for children facilitate play

Discover the causes for deterioration in downtown areas

Find out how light influences the shape of spaces

Examine the relationship of sounds in the environment

Examine the urban planning process

Examine the relationship between climate and comfort

Examine how zoning ordinances influence the quality of the visual environment

Find out how we can reuse our built environment

Examine local legislative issues which affect public planning decisions

Examine how different surfaces look and feel

Examine sources of pollution in the built environment

Discover how we communicate with color

Examine public transportation in your city

Examine how buildings are constructed in your community

Examine how people's movement suggests the shape of spaces

Discover how open and closed spaces effect your feelings

Examine how buildings are supported and enclosed

Examine the relationship between how people live and how they build

instructions

This board game is to be played by a group of 3–5 people. Each step begins with individual choices, followed by group discussion to decide upon a group choice. As group discussion begins, players should be urged to enthusiastically support their individual choices until they persuade, or are persuaded by others, that a single choice should be adopted for the group.

Step 1. To begin, each player selects the LEARNING OBJECTIVE which he feels is the most important from the list on the right. (You can use this list to make a "deck" of objective cards, adding objectives which you believe should be considered.) Players then discuss their choices and select from their individual decisions a group choice. Place the final card on the board in the LEARNING OBJECTIVE spot.

Step 2. Each player now chooses one ENVIRONMENTAL TOPIC which he/she feels is most important when working with students. Discuss the choices as a group—once again with all individual choices exposed to all— then place the card which corresponds to your group choice in the topic box.

Step 3. Using the environmental topic as the basis for your choices, individually choose 3 ACTIVITIES. Pooling your choices, agree as a group on 3 activities, then place the cards face up in the appropriate box on the game board.

Step 4. Refer to the LEARNING OBJECTIVE on the game board and decide on 3 LEARNING METHODS which will best support your objective. Discuss as a group. Place 3 choices on the game board.

Step 5. Now take a close look at what has been chosen. The relationships between all elements of the process may be seen in the matrix which has been created in the last square of the game board. Use these combinations of ideas generated as a starting point for group activities or a lesson plan.

Step 6. When you have decided upon appropriate group projects—either for the players of the board game or for a larger group such as a class—follow through with a systematic evaluation of the activities you carry out. You can use the worksheet on the next page as a possible model for your evaluation. See how well your game decisions matched up with the project results.

learning methods

Act out situations
Group problem solving
Identify and talk to experts
Participate in changing the environment
Question people's attitudes
Express how you feel
Search for existing information
Communicate your findings to others
Represent your ideas graphically
Observe people's behavior in the environment
Describe environmental settings

learning objectives

Stimulating and encouraging imagination
Developing curiosity and encouraging resourcefulness
Stimulating and encouraging resourcefulness
Developing problem solving skills
Experiential learning
Developing technical skills
Developing motivation for learning
Developing initiative and spontaneity
Developing student's sense of community identity
Developing perceptual acuity
Encourage student's sense of reality
Developing social awareness
Encourage communication skills
Developing sense of responsibility
Developing self-expression
Encouraging a sense of responsibility

environmental topics

Modifying and changing the built environment through sensory experience
Knowing the environment effect our activities
How does our environment, and make our environment
People who use, design, and build
Systems in the built environment
Factors which influence the form of our environment
Relationship between the natural and built environment

environmental education game

LEARNING OBJECTIVES	Statements that describe the desired characteristics to be achieved by each child.	PROJECT WORKSHEET

ACTIVITIES	Statements describing the activities children will be involved in to accomplish the learning objectives.	Conditions necessary to perform tasks.

METHODS OF PRESENTATION	Statements of the methods student activities will be recorded and presented.	Materials necessary to perform tasks.

EVALUATION CRITERIA	Statements that describe the method of evaluating student work.

A worksheet for planning and evaluating group environmental projects.

ENVIRONMENTAL MEANING — 1

objectives To directly experience such comcepts as scale, contour, plan, elevation, and topograghic representation in an easily manipulated form.

activities

Stage 5.
The design of project proposals

Each student group was given a topographic map (1 inch=10 feet) and were asked to draw to scale their design propocals. By using the topograghic maps they were able to make full scale models of the elevational changes occuring on the site. From these models they were able to determine how to grade the site to accommodate their designs and how the elevational changes would effect the existing vegetation and drainage patterns of the site. The models were composed of layers of cardboard on styrofoam supports following an elevational scale of 1 inch = 5 feet. The students used plaster of Paris on a chicken wire base for the dome used to represent an inflatable dome to cover the football field during winter months of the year. Natural greenery was employed to indicate site vegetation. The models were then diplayed for the inspection of the entire school.

vocabulary
scale
cut and fill
plan
elevation
topograghic map
run off
erosion

materials
chicken wire
plaster of Paris
paint
syrofoam sheets
cardboard sheets
glue
cedar twigs
pipe cleaners
rasp, files, coping saws

ENVIRONMENTAL MEANING — 5

objectives To acquaint the children with the purpose and to allow them to explore land use alternatives.

activities

Stage 1.
(1) Introduced the project to the students
(2) Voted for a project name ("In Search of the Golden Fleece" was decided)
(3) Brainstormed for land use alternatives
(4) Grouped these uses into similar activity regions
(5) Students experienced the site directly

vocabulary
long range land planning
land use accessment
land use management
user needs

materials

ENVIRONMENTAL MEANING — 6

objectives Introduction of long range planning and land use management to the class. How are the visual appearances and activities that take place on different plots of land similar and dissimilar? How does the cost of land effects its use?

activities

Stage 2.
Cliff Hardy, the dirctor of the Housing Authority of Raliegh, spoke to the class about the site location and boundaries. He explained the concept of zoning and usage of the land surrounding the site. Mr. Hardy discussed the price the school paid for the land and how that price compared to land cost on the commercial market. He also explained that land was sold to the school with the understanding that the land had to be used for some purpose associated with the activities and functions of the school.

vocabulary
planner
zoning

materials

ENVIRONMENTAL MEANING — 7

objectives To familiarize the students with technical equipment and methods employed by professionals in land use assessment planning. To provide the students with a practical understanding of user needs and methods of participation.

activities

Stage 3.
The students were divided into work groups of five members each and roled played as the professionals associated with land use assessment and participatory planning.

(1) The "foresters" group were lead by a botonist to identify trees and select samples for herbarium sheets. They checked for the rarity of the tree specie, the health of the tree, measured the diameter of the tree, and determine which trees should be preserved if the land would be developed.

(2) The students participating as surveyers were accompanied by a professional surveyer to measure the site, calculate the square footage and the location of the trees on the site. From this information they were able to make a map of the site.

(3) The students participating as soil scientists were accompanied by a landscape student and tested the fertility of the soil to determine which agricultural and decorative plants would live in the soil in its present condition. They conducted an acid level test, a phosphorous test, a potash test, and a nitrogen test with a chemical soil testing kit on various locations of the site. They tested for bedrock to determine how far down for foundations for any proposed structure. They analyzed the slope using a toptgraghic map of Raleigh

vocabulary
user (who is he?)
user needs
surveyer
herbarium sheets
slope
nitrogen, phosphorous, potash, and acid level

materials
surveyers's transit and rod
chemical soil testing kit
soil bedrock and core tester
tree tape (for measuring tree diameters)

Project worksheets designed for a sixth grade center

DESCRIPTIVE WORDS

Active-Passive
ADEQUATE SIZE-INADEQUATE SIZE
Affected-Unaffected
Alive-Dead
APPEALING-UNAPPEALING
Ascending Color-Receding Color
ATTRACTIVE-UNATTRACTIVE
BEAUTIFUL-UGLY
BRIGHT-DULL
BRIGHT COLORS-MUTED COLORS
Busy-Calm
Calming-Upsetting
Changeable-Unchangeable
CHEERFUL-GLOOMY
CLEAN-DIRTY
Coarse-Smooth
COLORFUL-DRAB
COMFORTABLE-UNCOMFORTABLE
COMFORTABLE TEMPERATURE-UNCOMFORTABLE TEMPERATURE
Complete-Incomplete
COMPLEX-SIMPLE
Confused-Clear
Consonant-Dissonant
CONTEMPORARY-TRADITIONAL
Content-Discontent
CONVENIENT-INCONVENIENT
Coordinated-Uncoordinated
Cozy-Monumental
Cultured-Uncultured
Dated-Timeless
Decorated-Stark
Deep-Shallow
Defined Space-Undefined Space
Definite Volume-Indefinite Volume
Depressing-Exhilarating
DIFFUSE LIGHTING-DIRECT LIGHTING
Dignified-Undignified
Directed-Undirected
DISTINCTIVE-ORDINARY
Downward Scale-Upward Scale
DRAFTY-STUFFY
Dry-Humid
Dynamic Space-Static Space
EFFICIENT-INEFFICIENT
ELEGANT-UNADORNED
EMPTY-FULL
Encouraging-Discouraging
Euphonious-Diseuphonious
Even Texture-Uneven Texture
Exciting-Unexciting
EXPENSIVE-CHEAP
Expressive-Unexpressive
Familiar-Unfamiliar
FASHIONABLE-UNFASHIONABLE
Fatiguing-Invigorating
Feminine-Masculine
Finished-Unfinished
FLASHY COLORS-SUBDUED COLORS
Flexible-Rigid
Formal-Informal
Formed-Formless
Fragile-Sturdy
FREE SPACE-RESTRICTED SPACE
FRESH ODOR-STALE ODOR
Friendly-Unfriendly
Frilly-Tailored
FUNCTIONAL-NONFUNCTIONAL
GAY-DREARY
Gentle-Brutal
Glaring-Unglaring
Good-Bad
GOOD ACOUSTICS-POOR ACOUSTICS
GOOD COLORS-BAD COLORS
GOOD LIGHTING-POOR LIGHTING
GOOD LINES-BAD LINES
Good Odor-Bad Odor
GOOD TEMPERATURE-BAD TEMPERATURE
GOOD VENTILATION-POOR VENTILATION
Graceful-Clumsy
Hard-Soft
Hard Texture-Soft Texture

Harmonious-Discordant
Healthy-Unhealthy
Heavy-Light
Heterogeneous-Homogeneous
High-Low
Honest-Dishonest
Horizontal Volume-Vertical Volume
Hospitable-Inhospitable
Hot-Cold
HUGE-TINY
Human Scale-Inhuman Scale
Imaginative-Unimaginative
Impersonal-Personal
IMPRESSIVE-UNIMPRESSIVE
Inner-directed-Outer-directed
Inspiring-Discouraging
Interesting-Uninteresting
INVITING-REPELLING
LARGE-SMALL
Lazy-Energetic
LIGHT-DARK
Livable-Unlivable
Lively-Dull
Long-Short
Meaningful-Meaningless
Mechanical Space-Nonmechanical Space
MODERN-OLD FASHIONED
MULTIPLE PURPOSE-SINGLE PURPOSE
Mystic-Nonmystic
Natural-Artificial
NEAT-MESSY
NEW-OLD
Nice-Awful
No Odor-Strong Odor
Open-Closed
ODERLY-CHAOTIC
ORGANIZED-DISORGANIZED
ORNATE-PLAIN
Orthodox-Unorthodox
PLEASANT-UNPLEASANT
PLEASANT ODOR-UNPLEASANT
Pleasing-Annoying
Plush-Austere
Polished-Unpolished
Popular-Unpopular
Positive-Negative
Pretentious-Unpretentious
PRIVATE-PUBLIC
Progressive-Conservative
Proportional-Unproportional
QUIET-NOISY
Real-Phony
Rectilinear-Curvilinear
Refined-Unrefined
Refreshing-Wearying
Regular-Irregular
Related-Unrelated
Relaxed-Tense
Reputable-Disreputable
Reserved-Uninhibited
Resonant-Flat
Restful-Disturbing
Restrained-Unrestrained
Restricted-Unrestricted
Reverent-Irreverent
Rhythmic-Unrhythmic
Rich-Poor
Rickety-Stable
Romantic-Unromantic
ROOMY-CRAMPED
Scenic-Unscenic
Sectionalized Space-Undifferentiated Space
Secure-Insecure
Sedate-Flamboyant
Sensitive-Insensitive
Sensual-Prim
Serene-Disturbed
Serious-Humorous
Shaped-Shapeless
Sharp-Blunt
Sincere-Insincere
Sociable-Unsociable
SOFT LIGHTING-HARSH LIGHTING
Soothing-Distracting
Sophisticated-Unsophisticated
SPARKLING-DINGY
Spiritual-Nonspiritual
Stereotyped-Unstereotyped
Sterile-Filthy

How we behave in a specific place depends somewhat upon how that place "feels" to us. But often, if we want to say what something feels like or means to us, we can have difficulty putting feelings into words.

Description can be very concrete and general; for example, Mr. Webster states that a house is a building to live in. Description can also be associative and specific since Mr. Webster's house can be roomy, old, livable, urban and beautiful, dark and cramped or whatever.

We believe that the environment has an important meaning for each of us although our associations about the environment may be different. Sometimes it is possible to understand a specific environment better if we free-associate or generate as many descriptive words that we can identify.

We have collected a large list of words and their opposites that are good environmental descriptors. Each pair of words can be used to describe your classroom, your house, your place of worship or any other environment you may choose. This new vocabulary can help you see and understand subtle and varied qualities about your built environment. Add to the list as you need—the possibilities are endless!

WHAT WORDS DESCRIBE THESE PLACES ?

DINING ROOM

1 2 3 4			1 2 3 4
1 2 3 4	RESTRICTED SPACE ●	FREE SPACE	1 2 3 4
1 2 3 4	UNPLEASANT ●	PLEASANT	1 2 3 4
1 2 3 4	CHEERFUL ●	GLOOMY	1 2 3 4
1 2 3 4	SINGLE PURPOSE ●	MULTI PURPOSE	1 2 3 4
1 2 3 4	COMFORTABLE ●	UNCOMFORTABLE	1 2 3 4
1 2 3 4	NOISY ●	QUIET	1 2 3 4
1 2 3 4	UNIMAGINATIVE ●	IMAGINATIVE	1 2 3 4
1 2 3 4	BORING ●	INTERESTING	1 2 3 4
1 2 3 4	HAPPY ●	SAD	1 2 3 4
1 2 3 4	UNFRIENDLY ●	FRIENDLY	1 2 3 4
1 2 3 4	ORDINARY ●	DISTINCTIVE	1 2 3 4
1 2 3 4	SIMPLE ●	COMPLEX	1 2 3 4
1 2 3 4	INVITING ●	REPELLING	1 2 3 4

19

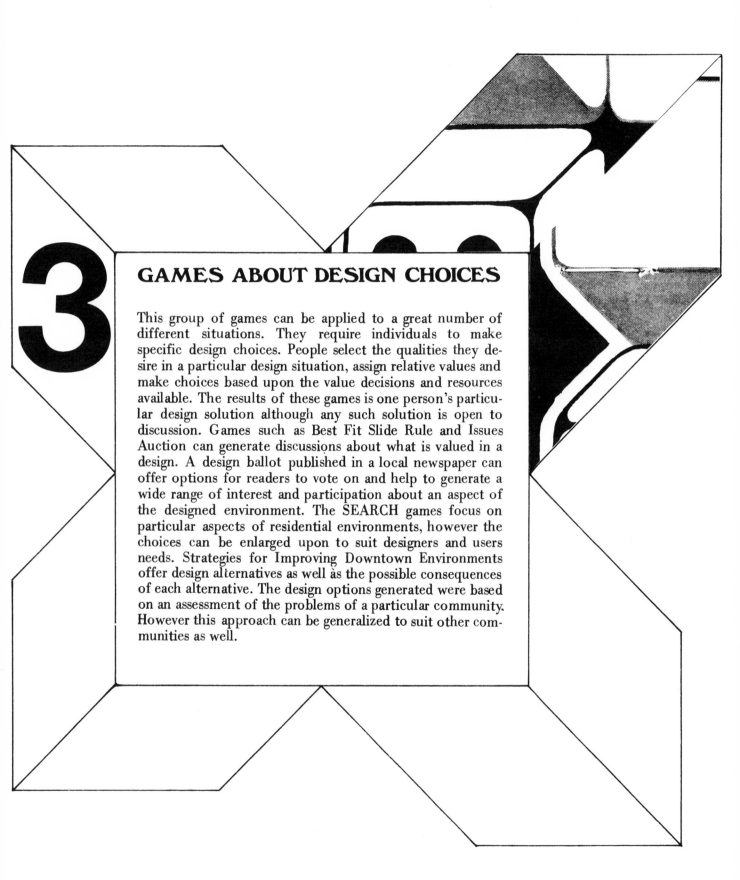

GAMES ABOUT DESIGN CHOICES

This group of games can be applied to a great number of different situations. They require individuals to make specific design choices. People select the qualities they desire in a particular design situation, assign relative values and make choices based upon the value decisions and resources available. The results of these games is one person's particular design solution although any such solution is open to discussion. Games such as Best Fit Slide Rule and Issues Auction can generate discussions about what is valued in a design. A design ballot published in a local newspaper can offer options for readers to vote on and help to generate a wide range of interest and participation about an aspect of the designed environment. The SEARCH games focus on particular aspects of residential environments, however the choices can be enlarged upon to suit designers and users needs. Strategies for Improving Downtown Environments offer design alternatives as well as the possible consequences of each alternative. The design options generated were based on an assessment of the problems of a particular community. However this approach can be generalized to suit other communities as well.

ISSUES AUCTION

The American Institute of Architects (AIA) has decided to choose the policy statement that they wish to support. An auction is being held where you are competing with others for the influence necessary to accomplish your policy statement. Only the issues bought at auction may be included in your priority list. For each item acquired, you are credited with the number of influence units originally set for the item, regardless of the amount paid. The goal is to acquire as many high priority items on your policy statement as possible. You have only 70 influence units to spend in the auction. Good luck! High score wins! Oh yes—the winner not only gets a big chance to change the future but also a $100,000 a year job at the AIA.

from Henry Sanoff, *Methods of Architectural Programming,* (Dowden, Hutchinson & Ross, 1977)

DIRECTIONS

From a set of design issues you and your colleagues are to select the seven that are most important in answering the question, WHAT MUST WE CONSIDER TO INCREASE THE RESPONSIVENESS OF THE BUILT ENVIRONMENT TO THE NEEDS OF PEOPLE?

Step 1. Make a deck of issues cards from the list at the right, adding any other issues which you would like to see discussed in the AIA policy meeting. Shuffle the deck.

Step 2. Each player has $100 to spend in the auction. Take up the issues one at a time from the deck and "bid" on them. High bidder for each issue takes that issue for his/her priority list. Continue bidding until the deck has been worked through or until every player has spent $100.

Step 3. Each player ranks the issues he or she purchased according to his/her priorities.

Step 4. Each player has 70 "influence points." Proceed around your conference table, discussing the first priority issues of each player. As issues come up, vote on them—one issue at a time—using influence points. Any of the players may vote for any of the issues which come up. Continue around the table again, voting on or until all of your "influence" is spent. When all of the voting is done, rank the top seven vote-getting issues. Those are the planks of your group policy statement: Good luck!

ISSUES

HOW DO WE CONSIDER AN INDIVIDUALS PSYCHOLOGICAL SPACE REQUIREMENTS

HOW PEOPLE MAINTAIN PRIVACY IN A CROWDED WORLD

RELATIONSHIP BETWEEN DENSITY AND CROWDING

EXPERIENCING COMPLEXITY IN THE BUILT ENVIRONMENT

HOW PEOPLE USE THE BUILT ENVIRONMENT TO ORIENT THEMSELVES

DO WE ATTRIBUTE MEANING TO COLOR

THE ATTRIBUTES OF ALIVE VERSUS DEAD SPACE

THE FIT BETWEEN THE ACTIVITIES WE PERFORM AND THE ENVIRONMENTS DESIGNED TO ACCOMMODATE THEM

HOW SPATIAL QUALITY EXPRESSES SOCIAL STATUS

HOW FURNITURE ARRANGEMENTS INFLUENCE SOCIAL INTERACTION

HOW DO WE DESCRIBE THE BUILT ENVIRONMENT

HOW SIMULATIONS CAN BE USED TO UNDERSTAND THE BUILT ENVIRONMENT

HOW DO WE EVALUATE THE QUALITY OF THE BUILT ENVIRONMENT

RELATIONSHIP BETWEEN FORM & FUNCTION

SPATIAL QUALITIES THAT DIFFERENTIATE PUBLIC FROM PRIVATE SPACE

RELATIONSHIP BETWEEN ENVIRONMENTAL FORM AND HUMAN BEHAVIOR

HOW LIGHT IS USED TO DEFINE SPACE

REUSING OLD BUILDINGS

RELATIONSHIP BETWEEN BUILDING DESIGN AND COMFORT

HOW THE SCALE OF OUR BUILT ENVIRONMENT AFFECTS PEOPLE

PROVISION OF OPTIONS IN THE BUILT ENVIRONMENT FOR SPECIAL POPULATIONS

INVISIBLE BOUNDARIES IN THE BUILT ENVIRONMENT

HOW PEOPLE PERSONALIZE THE SPACE THEY INHABIT

USER PARTICIPATION IN THE DESIGN PROCESS

HOW PEOPLE DEFEND THEIR TERRITORY AGAINST INVASION BY OTHERS

HOUSE FORM AND ITS RELATIONSHIP TO CULTURE

RELATIONSHIP BETWEEN DENSITY AND ACCESS TO AVAILABLE RESOURCES

HOW 'CUES' FROM THE BUILT ENVIRONMENT AFFECT US

HOW TO IDENTIFY USER PERCEPTIONS ABOUT THE BUILT ENVIRONMENT

RELATIONSHIP BETWEEN HUMAN MEASUREMENTS AND THE DIMENSIONS OF THE BUILT ENVIRONMENT

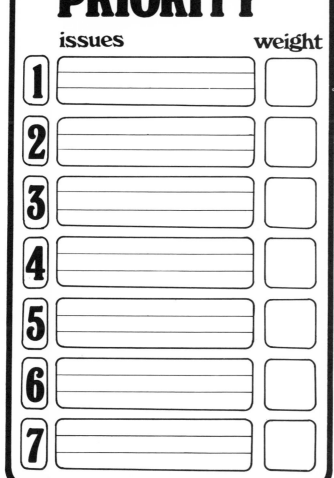

PRIORITY

	issues	weight
1		
2		
3		
4		
5		
6		
7		

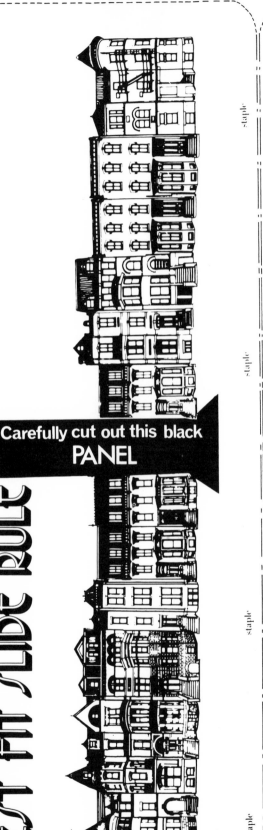

Carefully cut out this black PANEL

BEST FIT SLIDE RULE

fold along this line

staple · staple · staple · staple

fold along these lines

DIRECTIONS:

This typical block face can be found in most communities where residential areas have remained unaltered for many decades. Today, neglect and rapid decay have placed many blocks of this type in need of replacement or repair. In order to insure that there is some continuity in the process of restoring older residential areas, it is often necessary to evaluate new building proposals very carefully. This is done by comparing each new proposal with specific criteria developed to insure the preservation of those unique qualities that make older buildings visually distinctive.

On your slide rule you will find a drawing of Front Street, a typical residential block in downtown SERGORP. One of the buildings has been condemned by SERGORP's building department because it is unsafe for occupancy. There are twelve proposals for reusing the site of the condemned building.

As an interested citizen it is your job to insure the selection of a proposal which will preserve Front Streets unique character. Using the criteria checklist provided, review each of the twelve design proposals and decide which proposal fits best within the available space. Only that proposal which satisfies all eight criteria can be considered acceptable.

CRITERIA CHECKLIST

Each proposal must be evaluated using the criteria below and must be similiar to the adjacent buildings regarding the following:

- alignment of window and door openings
- relative height
- roof silhouette
- proportion of window and door openings
- use of ornamentation
- building use
- surface variation
- relative width

CUT THIS SLIDE RULE

Use these extra pages to cut out your own Best Fit Slide Rule.

staple

staple

staple

staple

Carefully cut out this black PANEL

BEST FIT SLIDE RULE

fold along this line

DIRECTIONS:

This typical block face can be found in most communities where residential areas have remained unaltered for many decades. Today, neglect and rapid decay have placed many blocks of this type in need of replacement or repair. In order to insure that there is some continuity in the process of restoring older residential areas, it is often necessary to evaluate new building proposals very carefully. This is done by comparing each new proposal with specific criteria developed to insure the preservation of those unique qualities that make older buildings visually distinctive.

On your slide rule 'you will find a drawing of Front Street, a typical residential block in downtown SERGORP. One of the buildings has been condemned by SERGORP's building department because it is unsafe for occupancy. There are twelve proposals for reusing the site of the condemned building.

As an interested citizen it is your job to insure the selection of a proposal which will preserve Front Streets unique character. Using the criteria checklist provided, review each of the twelve design proposals and decide which proposal fits best within the available space. Only that proposal which satisfies all eight criteria can be considered acceptable.

CRITERIA CHECKLIST

Each proposal must be evaluated using the criteria below and must be similiar to the adjacent buildings regarding the following:

- alignment of window and door openings
- relative height
- roof silhouette
- proportion of window and door openings
- use of ornamentation
- building use
- surface variation
- relative width

staple

staple

staple

staple

fold along these lines

ASSEMBLY INSTRUCTIONS

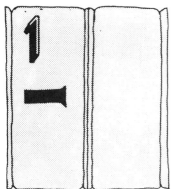

1 Remove the previous page from the workbook. Cut the slide rule out along the dotted lines which run along its outside edge. Then, carefully cut out the black panel as indicated.

2 Using a ruler as a guide, fold along the dotted and dashed lines (—·—·—·—). Use this picture to determine the direction of your folds.

3 Then fold the front and back panels together, insuring that the tabs are sandwiched between the two panels.

4 Staple where indicated, along both edges of your slide rule.

5 Cut out the strip (on this page) along the dotted lines and paste it to a piece of cardboard. Cut off any excess cardboard if necessary And, insert this strip into the slot. Read the directions and you're ready to go!

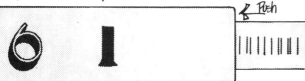

6 1 ← Push

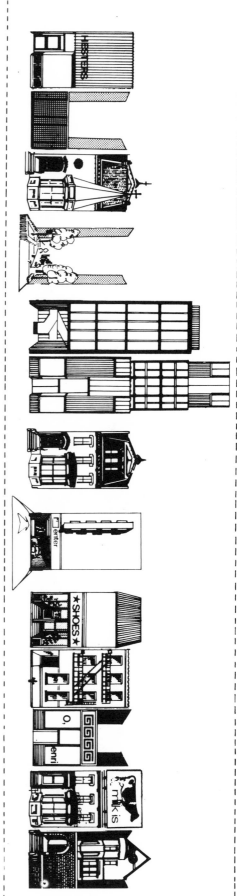

From Henry Sanoff, *Designing with Community Participation,* (Dowden, Hutchinson & Ross, 1978)

27

CUT THIS SLIDE RULE

ASSEMBLY INSTRUCTIONS

1

Remove the previous page from the workbook. Cut the slide rule out along the dotted lines which run along its outside edge. Then, carefully cut out the black panel as indicated.

Using a ruler as a guide, fold along the dotted and dashed lines (———·———·———). Use this picture to determine the direction of your folds.

2

3

Then fold the front and back panels together, insuring that the tabs are sandwiched between the two panels.

Staple where indicated, along both edges of your slide rule.

4

5

Cut out the strip (on this page) along the dotted lines and paste it to a piece of cardboard. Cut off any excess cardboard if necessary And, insert this strip into the slot. Read the directions and you're ready to go!

6 I

↖ Push

from Henry Sanoff, *Designing with Community Participation,* (Dowden, Hutchinson & Ross, 1978)

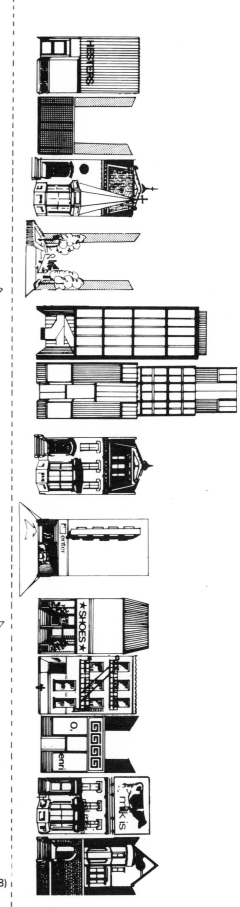

29

An illustration of alternative solutions possible through the manipulation of the slide

east side, south elm

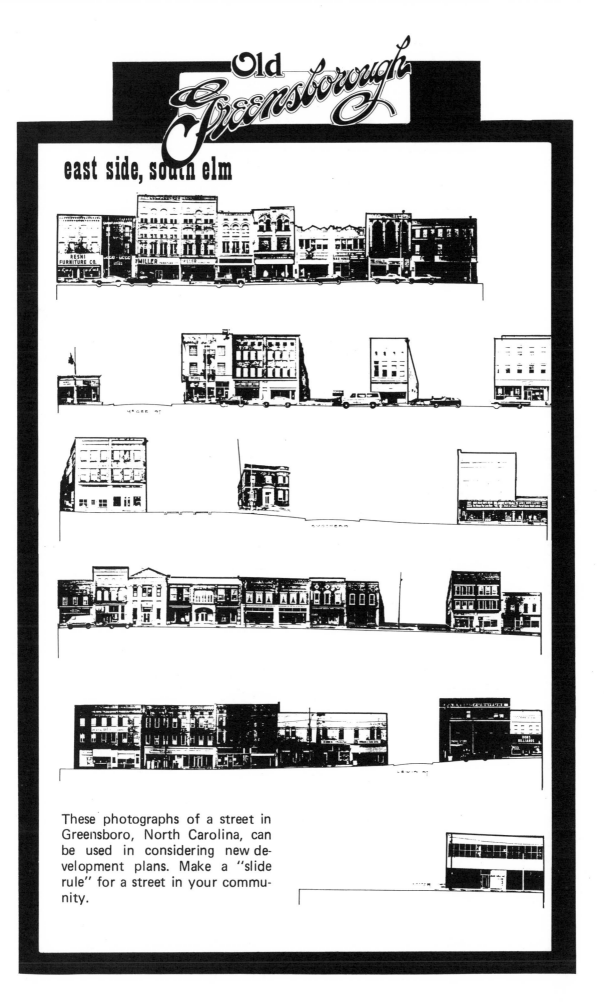

These photographs of a street in Greensboro, North Carolina, can be used in considering new development plans. Make a "slide rule" for a street in your community.

A DESIGN BALLOT FOR PUBLIC PARTICIPATION

Designer Lists Ways Old High School Could Be Used

The group of Farmville citizens interested in finding out what others in town think about restoring the old high school property postponed plans for a straw vote, in conjunction with Tuesday's election, until the public had been given results of a study and survey made by Richard Andrews of the North Carolina State University School of Design.

Andrews cited the following propositions:

- Renovating and adapting the old Farmville School for a community activity center would be cheaper than building a new community activity center.
- The old Farmville School may be placed on the National Historic Register. This makes renovation work eligible for federal funding.
- Funding to restore old buildings is easier to obtain than funding for new buildings.
- Renovating and adapting the old Farmville School would preserve a landmark with which many citizens identify.
- The existing building could be renovated and adapted to house:

A farmers' market	Public offices
Privately rented offices	Arts & crafts classrooms
Cafes	Scout meetings
A visitors' center	Civic club meetings

- The old Farmville School auditorium could be renovated and adapted for a little theater, a community concert hall, and a community meeting hall.
- Renovating and adapting the old Farmville School cafeteria would create space for community suppers, the elderly citizens' lunch program, fund raising dinners, and civic organization meetings.
- The old Farmville School gymnasium could become a town center for recreation, community dances, and art displays.
- The addition of a new community activity center would add more diversity to Farmville life, making it a more interesting place to live.
- Housing new activities in a renovated Farmville School would enliven the entire area, thus benefitting the adjacent downtown business.

Persons interested in the proposals are invited to state their positions on the following and return the forms to The Enterprise office on North Main Street or to mail their opinions to The Enterprise, Box 247, Farmville. No signatures are required, and the poll is an unofficial way of finding out if the town is interested in restoring the school, to what extent they are interested, and just how they feel about the restoration proposal.

The Commissioners have already received bids on demolishing the structures (the main building, the gymnasium and the agricultural building). The [illegible] agreed not to take final action until those [illegible] restoration have had time to complete [illegible] their recommendations. The lo[illegible] structures was $34,300.

Controversy Swirls Around Old School

The straw ballot which appeared in last week's Enterprise drew more responses than had been anticipated when the decision was made to print the proposals and ask for opinions about the old high school property.

A reply came from a former Farmville resident who now lives in Columbia, S. C.; another came from an ex-Farmville citizen who now lives in Richmond, Va.

The comments were interesting.

"Renovate the old school," demanded one.

To the first statement (The old Farmville school does not mean anything to Farmville's citizens. It should be demolished and a municipal building constructed on the site.), one commented, "This question is misleading. It does mean something to the citizens but what other site is there in Farmville?"

From Gina Allen Smith in Columbia, S. C., came this: "The school renovating plan is an exciting challenge. Do something about it."

Said another who disagreed with all six proposals: "Keep the only thing that has helped downtown Farmville looking decent and helped our merchants. When you moved the school, children and teachers from uptown, Farmville has looked and been a dead place to us citizens and outsiders. That is why people go out as you are not helping our uptown business men. You're all for se[illegible] and taxes."

Said another, [illegible] old school b[illegible] an[illegible] novate for [illegible]ny uses."

To [illegible] Farmville [illegible] facilities [illegible] activities which [illegible] be [illegible]sed in a [illegible] center," one [illegible] asked "Where?" and [illegible]ded, [illegible]st destruction [illegible] school."

Another [illegible] as follows:

The[illegible] things to be disc[illegible] decision sh[illegible] made about [illegible] use of [illegible] old Farmville [illegible]tral High School Building [illegible] a pity to demolish buildings that are useful and with possible repair and alteration of structure could be made useful to a community. Certainly there are many worthwhile suggestions given by Mr. Andrews of the North Carolina State University School of Design but it is difficult for the average citizen to fill out the form given in the Enterprise when all the facts are not known. For example: how many of the citizens of this community actually know whether the community center truly serves the needs of its citizens? Are there activities for the elderly now as part of the recreational program of the town? If there are facilities, is there a person who could head up such a program or would this too come under the supervision of the Recreation Director? How badly is a municipal building needed by the community? If the school is torn down, are there plans now in formation to build such a municipal building? What is the possibility of combining some municipal offices with other parts of the building used for community activities? All these and many more questions come to mind as opinions are gathered and decisions are made.

Judging from persons with whom I have talked or heard discussing the old Farmville school site, i[illegible] certainly considered a [illegible] mark for many. It would [illegible] to our cred[illegible] day of re-thinki[illegible] considering [illegible] as a commu[illegible] the vision and [illegible] challenge to renov[illegible] and use existing structures [illegible] rather than to [illegible] re-build.

Rom W[illegible] sta[illegible] L[illegible] a[illegible] [illegible] school [illegible] so [illegible]tal that we are b[illegible] by t[illegible]s of sorrow. [illegible] graduated from this sch[illegible] but I will not shed a tear if it is torn down because it would be a financial albatross around our necks to restore the building for any purpose.

Even if it was restored at no cost to the taxpayer, the yearly upkeep would be a burden that I would not want our children and grandchildren to pay.

Since we already own it—much to my regret—let's tear it down, straighten out Belcher and Grimmersburg streets, and turn the rest of the property into a Town Common.

From Lucy Rumley, one of the leaders in the move to get the Commissioners to postpone final action on the school until studies could be made as to the building's restoration, has this comment:

"Among the many responses which I have received inthe past two weeks concerning efforts to save our old school building are two which I think are especially important because they concern school buildings very similar to our school building. These buildings are just two of the many which communities are now taking the trouble and expense to save.

"The first item is a picture from the Boston Evening Globe for September 27, 1977, which shows a picture of the Palmer School in Needham, Mass., which was slated for demolition but is now slated to become housing for the elderly. This clipping came to me through the courtesy of Arthur Jones.

"The second article is in the September issue of 'Southern Living.' It shows a picture of a school building in Charlottesville, Va., which closely resembles our old building. This building has been renovated into the McGuffey Art Center. This article was called to my attention by my sister-in-law, Mrs. Cecil Johnston. after it was called to her attention by Mrs. Jack Lewis. Lewis."

The articles contained pictures of the buil[illegible]s and one of them i[illegible] remarkably like the ol[illegible] [illegible]le high school.

School Is Given Reprieve; Board Delays Plans

Appearing Tuesday night before the Board of Commissioners, local citizens who are not convinced that the old high school buildings on North Main Street are ready for the scrap heap won a reprieve for the doomed structures and were assured their opinions, and the results of a study they are making, will be considered before final action is taken.

Bids [illegible] demolishing the buildin[illegible] [illegible]ned on O[illegible] [illegible] [illegible]bulation [illegible] Commissioners [illegible]ht. D. H. [illegible]ffin [illegible] Greensboro [illegible] [illegible] [illegible]ar down [illegible] high school building[illegible] [illegible] agricultural b[illegible] gymna[illegible] [illegible]300. R[illegible] [illegible] [illegible]mond, [illegible] to [illegible] work fo[illegible] the [illegible] bid for tea[illegible] [illegible] the high scho[illegible] building, alone, was $24,0[illegible].

Mrs. Lucy Rumley, who has served as one of the leaders and spokesman of a group hoping the main building can be restored and put to good use by the town, told the Commissioners she was not sentimentally attached to the structure, although she went to school there, but she felt the buildings should not be torn down until restorers had inspected it, and determined to what uses it could be put. She cited the town's need for suitable meeting places. Mrs. Rumley said if an impartial study showed costs of restoration unreasonable, she would agree the buildings should be torn down and would heartily support the board's decision to order the demolition. She added, however, that persons from State University had looked at the building, and were evaluating their findings. She asked the board to postpone the decision for possibly as long as six months until adequate studies are made.

Mrs. Grace Carraway, another of the delegation hoping the buildings can be restored and put to good use, said the presence of old, restored buildings enhaned a town's appearance. W. A. Allen said the town would be better off by restoring the building, if it was not too costly, rather than tearing down the structures and having vacant lots.

As soon as the matter came up for discussion Commissioner W. R. Duke asked that the question be postponed. He said he could not, in good conscience vote to accept the bids and to order the buildings demolished until additional studies had been made.

Commissioner Jack Farrior cited the results of an inspection by a top engineer with the State Insurance Department who listed the improvements required before the building could be converted to public use. Farrior said the costs of maintaining, heating and cooling the building were almost prohibitive, much more than they would be for an efficiently built structure.

The board's action evidently voids the bids received on October 25 since Town Administrator Pat Thomas informed the Commissioners, via memo that they had 30 days from the date of opening to accept the bids.

Mayor Will Joyner presided over the session. Present were all members of the board: Mrs. Sara Albritton, Duke, Farrior, Durwood Little and John Turner Walston.

Planning, Design Group Studies Local Building

A planning and design group in Raleigh has offered its services to the Town of Farmville for a study of the old school property.

The Community Development Group which provides technical assistance for individual and community projects that cannot afford these services is headed by Henry Sanoff. Mr. Sanoff is the Director of the School of Design at N. C. State University. The group has aided in projects across North Carolina, including ones in Cary, Salisbury, Lumberton and Murfreesboro.

In Farmville, members of the Group would assist by surveying the structure of the main school building for soundness, gathering ideas for alternative uses of the building and re-designing the space to accommodate the uses. Through their work, a determination of the community's need for the space in the building will be made. If a need exists, an estimate can be made of the costs of any action.

Mr. Sanoff and the Community Development Group have helped many small communities take advantage of the resources at hand and hope to assist Farmville in a thorough examination of the possibilities for the old school property.

Straw Votes On School Will Be Taken Tuesday

An opinion survey concerning the old school property will be taken outside the polling area on Tuesday, Nov. 8.

Citizens will be asked to state their preference as to the future of the main school building.

The ballot will read: With relation to the old school property on Main Street, which action would you rather have taken: if feasible, restore the main school building; tear the main school building down and build a municipal complex; no opinion.

The results of the survey should help the town to decide what to do with the property.

PUBLIC PARTICIPATION

Frequently communities are involved in environmental projects that require some form of citizen response or reaction. Recognizing that public meetings only attract the more vocal community residents, a ballot was conceived as a way to involve many people in reacting to an environmental issue.

The ballot illustrated consists of propositions outlining alternative proposals for the future of a vacant building and statements dealing with community activities that could influence new uses for the building. Together, these parts of the ballot provide the citizens with a method to express their feelings.

Old Farmville School

SAVE ?

INTRODUCTION

The old Farmville School is in danger of being demolished! A municipal building is proposed to be constructed on the site.

Isn't it about time that somebody asked you what you want to do or see happen with the school?

We think your positions can help everyone interested decide the fate of the old Farmville School.

INSTRUCTIONS

The old Farmville School survey raises some important questions that we need to answer. The following information will help you to form your own opinion about what should be done with the old Farmville School.

After carefully reading the first four sections, use the spaces provided either to agree or to disagree with the statements in the previous section.

ISSUES

The old Farmville School is more than just an old building. It is a landmark with which many of us identify. Because the building is old doesn't mean that it should be destroyed It could be renovated and converted to serve Farmville as a community activity center. Renovating and converting the building would reflect Farmville's conservative spirit while preserving an important part of the towns' heritage.

PROPOSITIONS

- Renovating and adapting the old Farmville School for a community activity center would be cheaper than building a new community activity center.

- The old Farmville School may be placed on the National Historic Register. This makes renovation work eligible for federal funding.

- Funding to restore old building is easier to obtain than funding for new buildings.

- Renovating and adapting the old Farmville School would preserve a landmark with which many citizens identify.

- The existing building could be renovated and adapted to house:

  Public offices A farmers' market
  Arts & crafts classrooms Privately rented offices
  Scout meetings Cafes
  Civic club meetings A visitor center

  The old Farmville School auditorium could be renovated and adapted for a little theater, a community concert hall, and a community meeting hall.

- Renovating and adapting the old Farmville School cafeteria would create space for community suppers, the elderly citizens' lunch program, fund raising dinners, and civic organization meetings.

- The old Farmville School gymnasium could become a town center for recreation, community dances, and art displays.

- The addition of a new community activity center would add more diversity to Farmville life, making it a more interesting place to live.

- Housing new activities in a renovated Farmville School would enliven the entire area, thus benefitting the adjacent downtown businesses.

STATEMENTS

1. The old Farmville School does not mean anything to Farmville's citizens. It should be demolished and a municipal building constructed on the site.

2. The old Farmville School site is the only one on which a new municipal building could be located.

3. The present recreation center already serves the entire needs of the community.

4. Farmville would benefit from a community center and the activities which it would house.

5. Farmville already has adequate facilities for the activities which might be housed in a community center

6. Downtown Farmville would not benefit from increased activity.

YOUR POSITION

1. AGREE _____ DISAGREE _____

2. AGREE _____ DISAGREE _____

3. AGREE _____ DISAGREE _____

4. AGREE _____ DISAGREE _____

5. AGREE _____ DISAGREE _____

6. AGREE _____ DISAGREE _____

A technique designed for examining urban planning propositions developed by the San Francisco Community Design Center

SEARCH

SYSTEMATIC EVALUATION OF ARCHITECTURAL REQUIREMENTS FOR COMMUNITY HOUSING

DESIGNED BY THE COMMUNITY DEVELOPMENT GROUP

SCHOOL OF DESIGN NORTH CAROLINA STATE UNIVERSITY

SEARCH is a collection of games, each one of which is designed to help establish user preferences for a set of intra and inter-dwelling characteristics. Game I, the Household Activities Game, deals with a set of floor arrangement of activity spaces. Game II, Plan Alternatives, is a set of floor plan variations. Game III, the House Profile, deals with the external appearance of dwelling. Game IV, Spatial Organization, investigates the characteristics of the dwelling unit arrangements.

SEARCH is intended to be used as a method of generating alternatives for housing design and planning. The games can be played with one client, or as in the case of a community housing project, with a number of representatives from the community. In either case the person administering the game should keep a written record of the decisions made by the player(s). It is recommended that a record of the decisions be kept when the preferences of a large group are to be considered. Such a data sheet should provide for the recording of the decisions made and the player's reasons for each decision.

SEARCH was designed by COMMUNITY DEVELOPMENT GROUP, the School of Design, North Carolina State University, Raleigh, North Carolina

Published by the North Carolina Agricultural Extension Service N. C. State University at Raleigh, North Carolina and the U. S. Department of Agriculture, Cooperating. State College Station, Raleigh, N. C. George Hyatt Jr., Director. Distributed in furtherance of the Acts of Congress of May 8 and June 30, 1914.

household activities

This game attempts to describe different preferences for interior room arrangements within the limits of an economic "budget." Each choice of arrangements has an associated point value (related to its cost) and the player is given a maximum limit on the number of points with which he can budget his choices. The possible choices are divided into the categories of living-dining-kitchen arrangements, and sleeping arrangements for adults and children. The living-dining-kitchen choices differ according to size and the amount of separation between each activity area. The sleeping choices differ according to size, separation of adult and child sleeping areas, and the possibility of a children's playspace. By limiting the points available to play the game, it is possible to encourage the player to make decisions based on the need for privacy between kitchen, living and dining, and the possibility of a child playspace. An additional choice of housing extras (with no point values) is also offered.

Cards 29a, 37d, and 37b display bedroom arrangements where the parents room can be elsewhere in the dwelling and not connected to the childrens bedrooms.

1. The possible choices are displayed in two sets. Set 1 includes the living-dining-kitchen arrangements. Set 2 includes the sleeping arrangements.

2. The player selects one living-dining-kitchen choice from the first set and one adult and child sleeping choice from the second set. The point value of each arrangement is displayed in the lower right hand corner of each picture and is followed by a letter to differentiate arrangements having the same point value. The total of the choices from the first and second sets cannot exceed 68 points.

3. If the total exceeds 68 points, the player must make alternative choices from either set until the total point value of the choices is less than or equal to 68 points.

Set 1   # Set 2

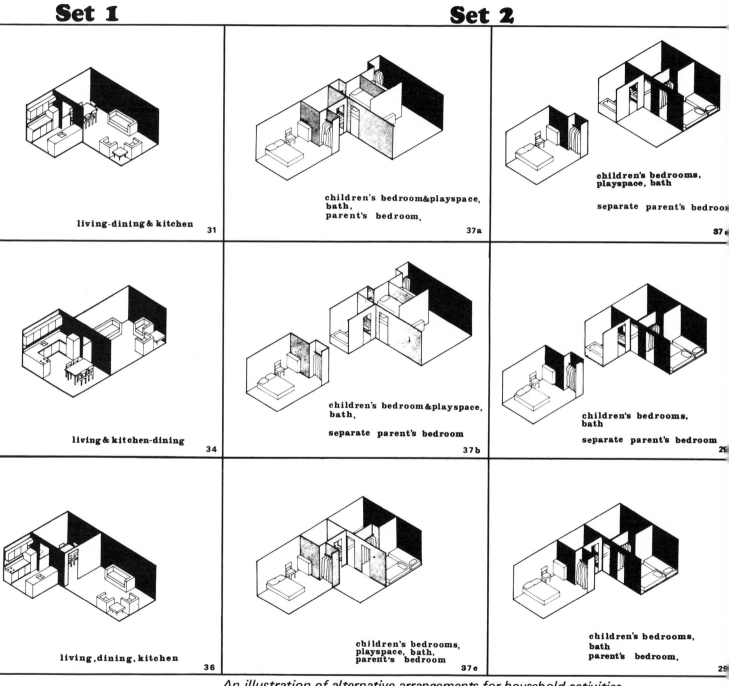

living-dining & kitchen   31

children's bedroom & playspace,
bath,
parent's bedroom,   37a

children's bedrooms,
playspace, bath

separate parent's bedroom   37

living & kitchen-dining   34

children's bedroom & playspace,
bath,

separate parent's bedroom   37b

children's bedrooms,
bath

separate parent's bedroom   2

living, dining, kitchen   36

children's bedrooms,
playspace, bath,
parent's bedroom   37c

children's bedrooms,
bath
parent's bedroom,   29

An illustration of alternative arrangements for household activities.

plan alternatives

This game describes eleven floor plan alternatives, all based upon approximately the same floor area. Each of the floor plans include three bedrooms, kitchen, bath, living, dining and some also include work or play areas. The alternatives suggest that families with different needs, desires, and life styles can be accomodated by careful design and planning. While each floor plan can easily include a front porch and incorporate modifications, choices should be made based on the information contained in the picture as well as the plans flexibility for accomodating changes.

1. The player should review the floor plans and be-come familiar with them.

2. The player selects the floor plan best suited for "child rearing."

3. The player selects the floor plan best suited for entertaining guests.

4. The player selects the floor plan best suited to, accomodate the "needs and desires of his family."

5. The player selects from the set of three, the best "all-around" floor plan.

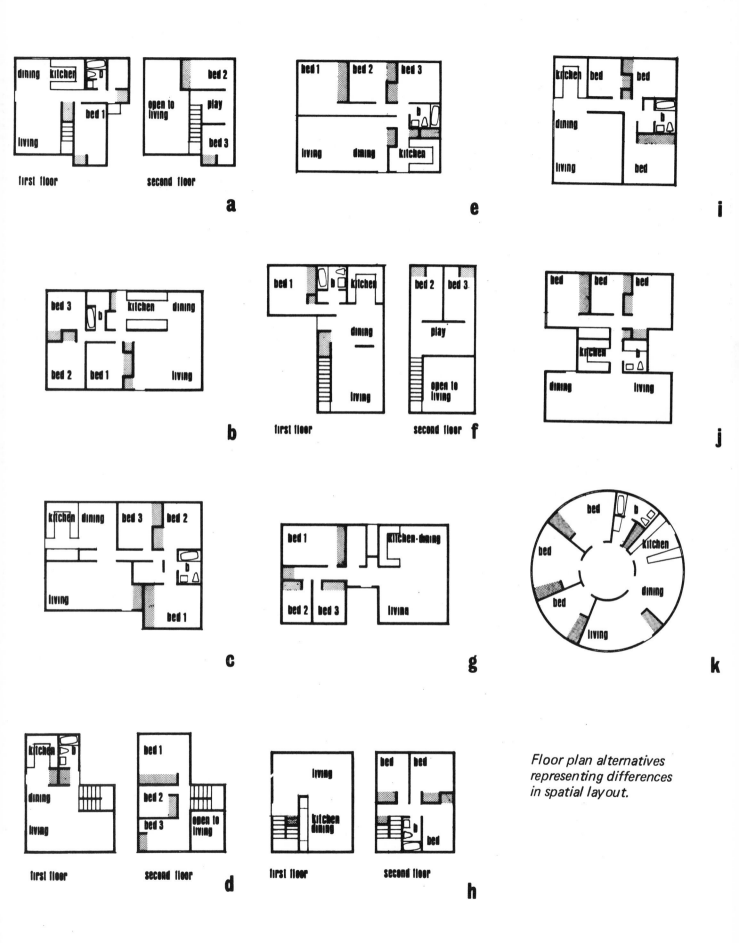

Floor plan alternatives representing differences in spatial layout.

39

house image

Game III is a collection of photographs representing a broad range of house types. Some of the twelve units pictured are typical tract homes, older conventional dwellings, and architect designed houses. A player's response to the appearance of a particular house type will be determined by what he has seen and is familiar with and also by those visual characteristics that he associates with the house in which he hopes to live. By making decisions about the visual array presented to him, the player is indicating the visual qualities that he desires in a home.

1. The player ranks the pictures in order of his preference, from 1 to 12.

2. The player is asked to describe the particular characteristics of his first two choices and the reasons for disliking choices 11 and 12.

B

C

E

F

H

I

K

L

41

site alternatives

This game attempts to describe preferences for a variety of inter-dwelling characteristics. These characteristics are functions of variation in the arrangement of the amount and type of open space (public and private), the arrangement of the units on the site, the amount and arrangement of parking space, and the number of floors per building. Each picture describes various types of parking arrangements, inter-dwelling privacy characteristics, outdoor child play spaces, outdoor family activities, and outdoor neighboring activities. While it is improbable that one particular organization of dwelling units will satisfy all a player's requirements, the decisions that a player makes will indicate the kind of spatial organization that would be desirable in any design solution.

1. The player should become familiar with each picture.
2. The player ranks the pictures in order of preference for "outdoor children's play areas."
3. The player ranks the pictures in order of preference for "inter-dwelling privacy."
4. The player ranks the pictures in order of preference for "outdoor family activities."
5. The player ranks the pictures in order of preference for "outdoor neighboring activities."
6. The player ranks the pictures in order of preference for "physical security."
7. The player ranks the pictures in order of preference for "visual appeal."
8. The player ranks the pictures in order of preference for the "best all-around arrangement."

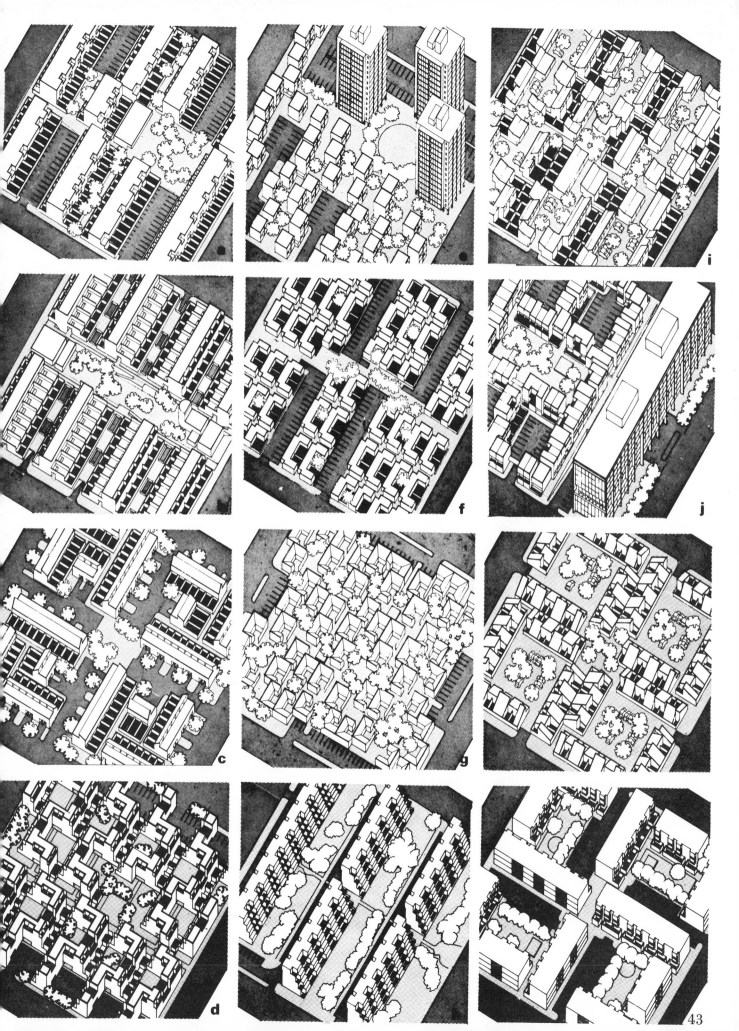

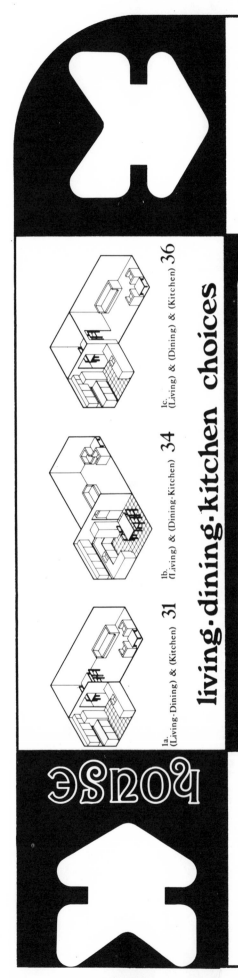

living·dining·kitchen choices

1a.
(Living·Dining) & (Kitchen) **31**

1b.
(Living) & (Dining·Kitchen) **34**

1c.
(Living) & (Dining) & (Kitchen) **36**

house choice

GAME OBJECT

The objective of this game is to select, from an array of cards, your preference of a living-dining-kitchen arrangement, two sleeping components (one adult and one children's), a "level" (one or two story) component, and a style (appearance) component without exceeding a total of 75 points.

GAME PROCEDURE

● Select a level (one or two story) preference and record point value on score sheet.

●● Select a style preference.

●● Select a living-dining-kitchen arrangement and record point value on score sheet.

● Select a parent's-bedroom preference and record point value on score sheet.

● Select a children's-bedroom preference and record point value on score sheet.

● Total the point value of selected preferences. If the total exceeds 75 points, initiate trial two by beginning with step (a). Record the choices and point values under the next "trial" column.

● The game concludes when the game objectives have been satisfied.

5b.
Two Story: (Interior)

5a.
Two Story: (Interior)

5d.
Two Story: (Exterior)

4c.
Two Story: (Exterior)

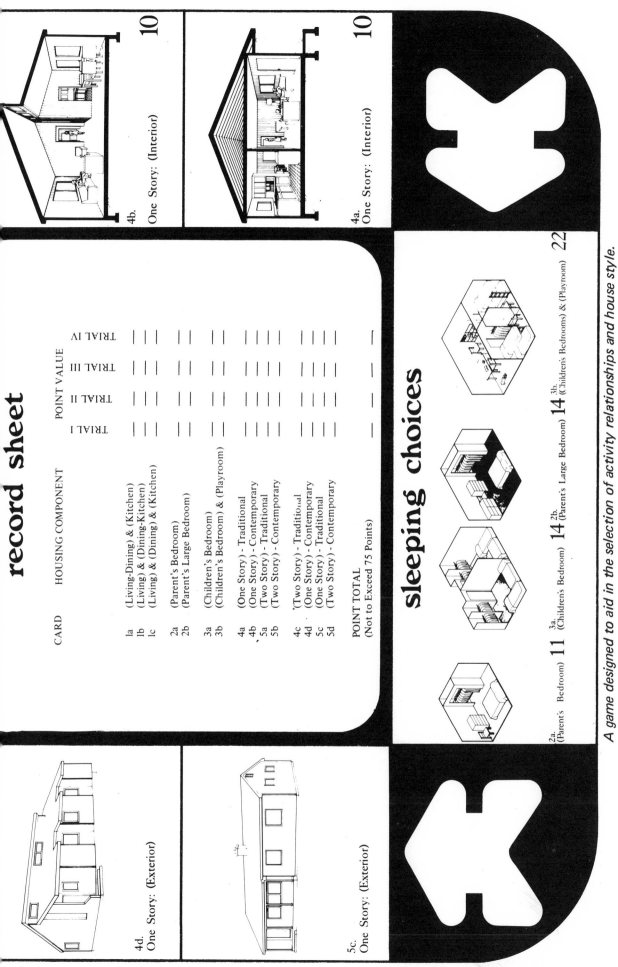

record sheet

CARD	HOUSING COMPONENT	POINT VALUE	TRIAL I	TRIAL II	TRIAL III	TRIAL IV
1a	(Living-Dining) & (Kitchen)					
1b	(Living) & (Dining-Kitchen)					
1c	(Living) & (Dining) & (Kitchen)					
2a	(Parent's Bedroom)					
2b	(Parent's Large Bedroom)					
3a	(Children's Bedroom)					
3b	(Children's Bedroom) & (Playroom)					
4a	(One Story) - Traditional					
4b	(One Story) - Contemporary					
5a	(Two Story) - Traditional					
5b	(Two Story) - Contemporary					
4c	(Two Story) - Traditional					
4d	(One Story) - Contemporary					
5c	(One Story) - Traditional					
5d	(Two Story) - Contemporary					
	POINT TOTAL (Not to Exceed 75 Points)					

4b. One Story: (Interior) 10

4a. One Story: (Interior) 10

4d. One Story: (Exterior)

5c. One Story: (Exterior)

sleeping choices

2a. (Parent's Bedroom) 11

3a. (Children's Bedroom) 14

2b. (Parent's Large Bedroom) 14

3b. (Children's Bedrooms) & (Playroom) 22

A game designed to aid in the selection of activity relationships and house style.

45

A game for downtown merchants and planners to discuss proposals and strategies for improving central business districts.

SIDE

strategies for improving downtown environments

1) Select three goals which you feel are important to downtown Murfreesboro. You may also propose your own goal. Individual sets of goals are then pooled and the four most important goals are selected by the group. You are encouraged to defend your choices until a mutually agreeable set of goals is obtained.

2) The group then chooses the three best strategies to achieve each goal. One strategy may be used more than once and you are again encouraged to propose your own. One goal is completed before the next is started, until the entire goal list is finished.

3) After all strategies are noted, you must try to anticipate the consequences of your actions. Hopefully, the result of the strategies will be the accomplishment of the goal. However, side effects may occur--making the downtown available for housing may also increase traffic. You must find two side effects for each strategy which could be either helpful or harmful. The list of side affects are then pooled. The group must decide which are most likely and delete the rest. Each side effect which conflicts with any goal selected by the group is marked.

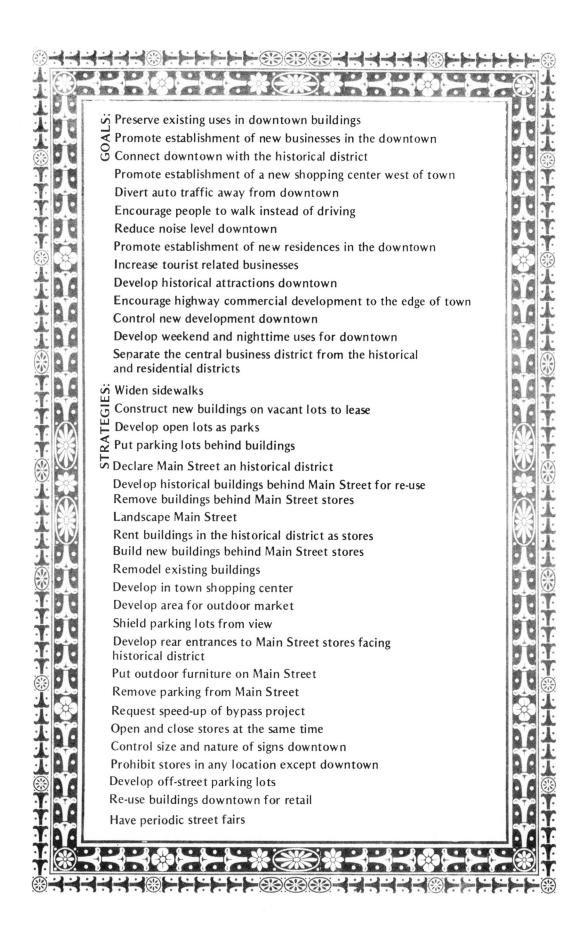

GOALS:

Preserve existing uses in downtown buildings

Promote establishment of new businesses in the downtown

Connect downtown with the historical district

Promote establishment of a new shopping center west of town

Divert auto traffic away from downtown

Encourage people to walk instead of driving

Reduce noise level downtown

Promote establishment of new residences in the downtown

Increase tourist related businesses

Develop historical attractions downtown

Encourage highway commercial development to the edge of town

Control new development downtown

Develop weekend and nighttime uses for downtown

Separate the central business district from the historical and residential districts

STRATEGIES:

Widen sidewalks

Construct new buildings on vacant lots to lease

Develop open lots as parks

Put parking lots behind buildings

Declare Main Street an historical district

Develop historical buildings behind Main Street for re-use

Remove buildings behind Main Street stores

Landscape Main Street

Rent buildings in the historical district as stores

Build new buildings behind Main Street stores

Remodel existing buildings

Develop in town shopping center

Develop area for outdoor market

Shield parking lots from view

Develop rear entrances to Main Street stores facing historical district

Put outdoor furniture on Main Street

Remove parking from Main Street

Request speed-up of bypass project

Open and close stores at the same time

Control size and nature of signs downtown

Prohibit stores in any location except downtown

Develop off-street parking lots

Re-use buildings downtown for retail

Have periodic street fairs

SIDE

strategies for improving downtown environments

goals	strategies	side effects

1. PROMOTES ESTABLISHMENT OF BUSINESSES

CONSTRUCT NEW BUILDINGS

PUT PARKING LOTS BEHIND BUSINESSES

NEED AGREEMENTS WITH PROPERTY OWNERS

PROBLEMS WITH WAREHOUSES BEHIND BUILDINGS

2. DIVERT TRUCK TRAFFIC

GET ON WITH NORTH BYPASS

RE-LOCATION OF BUSINESS

LOSS OF BUSINESS TO GAS STATION AND RESTAURANTS

3. CONTROL DOWNTOWN DEVELOPMENT AS TO TYPE AND NATURE OF BUSINESSES

PROHIBIT STORES IN ANY AREA EXCEPT DOWNTOWN

REMOVE EXISTING BUILDINGS

MAY NEED TO MODIFY (ZONING) LAWS

COST FACTOR, MAY INFRINGE ON FREE ENTERPRISES

A record sheet showing the results recorded by a group of merchants indicating their priorities for improving the local business district.

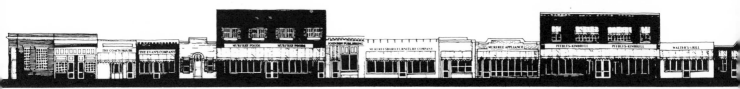

BUILD NEW BUILDINGS BEHIND MAIN STREET STORES

DEVELOP OPEN LOTS AS PARKS

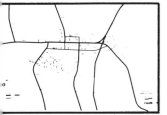

REQUEST SPEED-UP OF BYPASS PROJECT

PUT PARKING LOTS BEHIND BUILDINGS

DEVELOP IN TOWN SHOPPING CENTER

DEVELOP REAR ENTRANCES TO MAIN STREET STORES FACING HISTORICAL DISTRICT

HAVE PERIODIC STREET FAIRS

RENT BUILDINGS IN THE HISTORICAL DISTRICT AS STORES

CONSTRUCT NEW BUILDINGS ON VACANT LOTS TO LEASE

SHIELD PARKING LOTS FROM VIEW

DEVELOP AREA FOR OUTDOOR MARKET

LANDSCAPE MAIN STREET

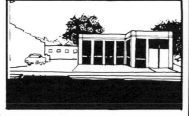

RE-USE BUILDINGS DOWNTOWN FOR RETAIL

WIDEN SIDEWALKS

comparison of proposed changes to a business district illustrating existing conditions and suggestions for improvements.

49

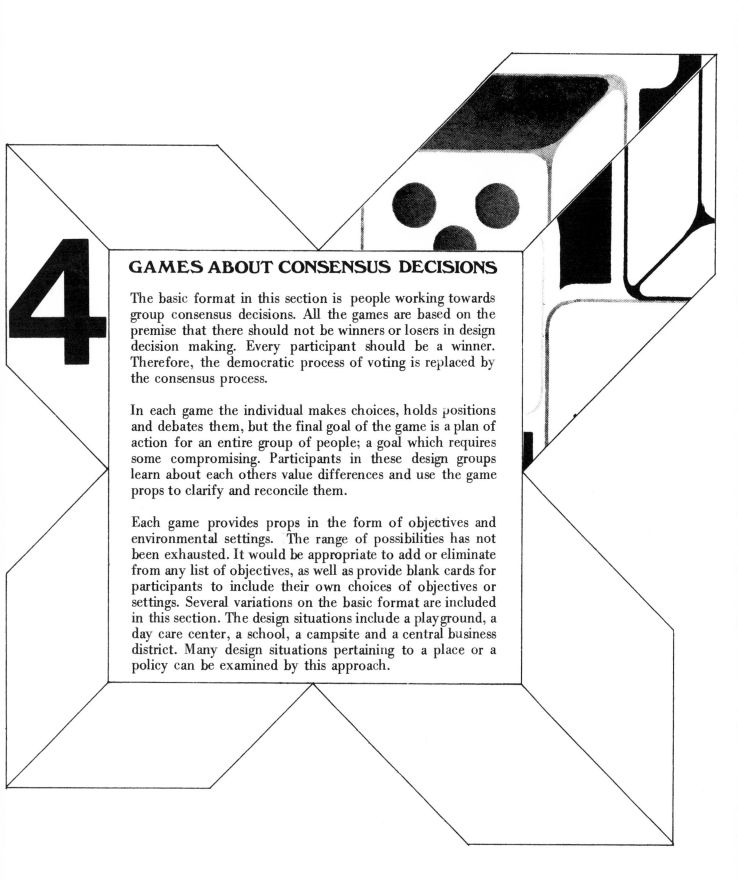

GAMES ABOUT CONSENSUS DECISIONS

The basic format in this section is people working towards group consensus decisions. All the games are based on the premise that there should not be winners or losers in design decision making. Every participant should be a winner. Therefore, the democratic process of voting is replaced by the consensus process.

In each game the individual makes choices, holds positions and debates them, but the final goal of the game is a plan of action for an entire group of people; a goal which requires some compromising. Participants in these design groups learn about each others value differences and use the game props to clarify and reconcile them.

Each game provides props in the form of objectives and environmental settings. The range of possibilities has not been exhausted. It would be appropriate to add or eliminate from any list of objectives, as well as provide blank cards for participants to include their own choices of objectives or settings. Several variations on the basic format are included in this section. The design situations include a playground, a day care center, a school, a campsite and a central business district. Many design situations pertaining to a place or a policy can be examined by this approach.

52

planning outdoor play
pop

from Henry Sanoff, *Designing with Community Participation*, (Dowden, Hutchinson & Ross, 1978)

Planning Outdoor Play (POP) is a method of facilitating the process of designing children's outdoor play areas and the selection of appropriate play equipment.

POP consists of four categories:

OBJECTIVES: the purpose of outdoor play
ACTIVITIES: the actions children engage in
ZONES: areas where related activities occur
SETTINGS: the location of children and the play equipment.

NOTE: You may prefer to make individual game cards for each item of the listed categories. The use of cards is a convenient way to manipulate the items so that they are accessible to the group.

The game can be played by small groups ranging in size from three to five people (teachers, parents, administrators).

pop

To begin, each player selects four of the most important OBJECTIVE statements. After each player has completed this step in the process, the individual selections are pooled. Through negotiation the group must agree on four acceptable OBJECTIVES that represent the spirit of the group. Players are urged to forcefully support their individual choices especially if other members did not make the same choice. The discussion should continue until they persuade or are persuaded by others that an OBJECTIVE should be included in the final set. Use the game record sheet to report the final decisions.

Next, as a group, examine each OBJECTIVE and select three ACTIVITIES that best satisfy each OBJECTIVE. Remember, more than one OBJECTIVE may be satisfied by the same ACTIVITY. Record all selections.

Now, as a group, rearrange all the ACTIVITY selections so they fit into an appropriate ZONE. It is important to note that not all of the ZONE cards need to be used. Record all selections.

Finally, select the appropriate SETTING that corresponds with each of the ACTIVITY choices and record the number of the SETTING.

This set of rules is only a guide for gaining insight into the planning process. Players should feel free to change the rules and equipment settings in order to accommodate more specific needs.

pop 1

Activities	Objectives
mixing	concept formation
feeling & handling	cooperation
hitting	problem solving
crawling	emotional development
splashing	self confidence
role playing	language development
dressing up	sensory discrimination
molding	self motivation
contact with animals	social development
digging	initiative
climbing	communication
painting	self expression
cooking	positive self image
pouring	perceptual development
stretching	sensory development
sliding	
constructing	
planting	
swinging	
throwing & catching	
balancing	
vehicular motion	

private play zone - children use small protected areas for individual or quiet activities.

dramatic play zone - children exercise their imaginations to create roles.

adventure play zone - children spontaneously build and rebuild their environment.

manipulative coordination zone - children develop coordination skills frequently with repetitive motion.

open area play zone - children use large spaces for group games and individual activities, which may require hard or soft surfaces.

creative play zone - children combine materials to make a different object.

large muscle development zone - children overcome physical and mental obstacles, exercising all possible muscles.

nature zone - children interact with natural objects.

imaginative play zone - children exercise imagination and limited muscular effort, but no object is necessarily produced.

pop 2

RECORD SHEET

OBJECTIVES

a _____
b _____
c _____
d _____

ACTIVITIES

a
1 _____
2 _____
3 _____

b
1 _____
2 _____
3 _____

c
1 _____
2 _____
3 _____

d
1 _____
2 _____
3 _____

pop 3

Equipment Settings

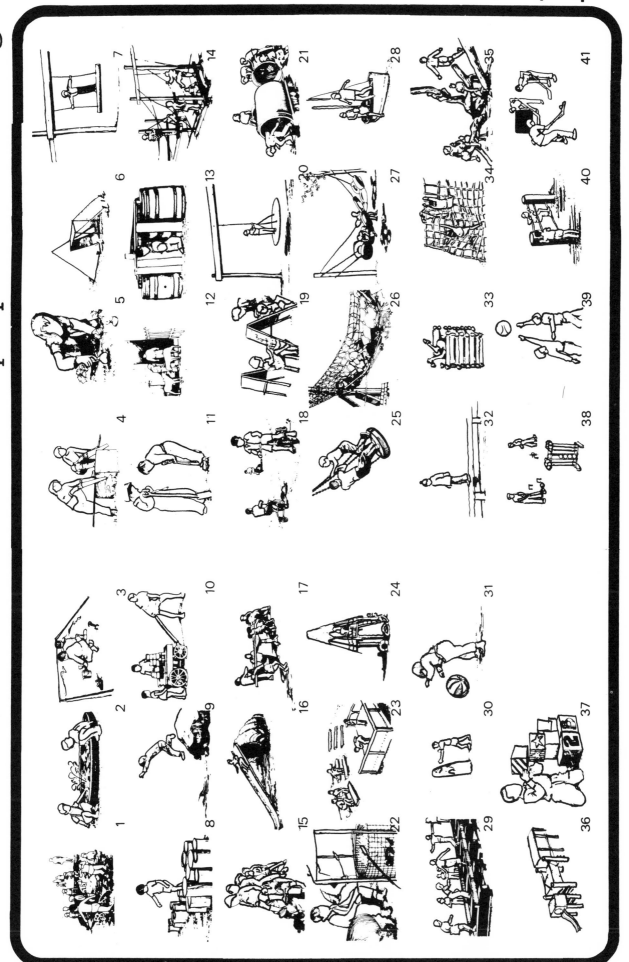

ZONES ACTIVITIES SETTINGS

Creative Play Zone

Imaginative Play Zone

Dramatic Play Zone

Nature Zone

Adventure Play Zone

Private Play Zone

Manipulative Coordination Zone

Large Muscle Development Zone

Open Area Play Zone

pop 5

Rules

1 Pick the four (4) most important OBJECTIVES for your playground.

☐   ☐   ☐   ☐

2 Select three (3) ACTIVITIES that satisfy the concept of each objective. Deal with one objective at a time.

☐   ☐   ☐   ☐
○ ○ ○   ○ ○ ○   ○ ○ ○   ○ ○ ○

3 Place each activity in the appropriate ZONE You may assign any number of activities to any of the zones.

○ ● ○ ● ○ ○ ○ ● ○
○ ○ ○ ○ ○ ○ ○ ○ G ○ ○ ○

4 Choose one (1) EQUIPMENT SETTING suitable for each activity.

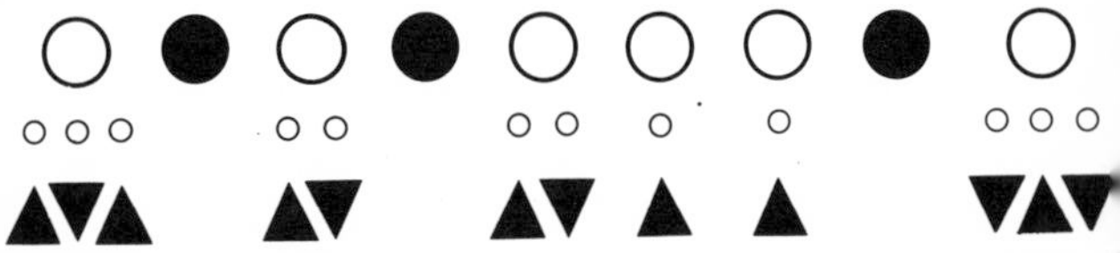

○ ● ○ ● ○ ○ ○ ● ○
○ ○ ○ ○ ○ ○ ○ ○ ○ ○ ○
▲▼▲ ▲▼ ▲▼ ▲ ▲ ▼▲▼

pop 6

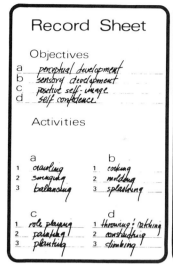

Record Sheet

Objectives

a perceptual development
b sensory development
c positive self-image
d self confidence

Activities

a
1 crawling
2 swinging
3 balancing

b
1 cooking
2 molding
3 splashing

c
1 role playing
2 painting
3 planting

d
1 throwing & catching
2 constructing
3 climbing

Zones	Activities	Equipment
Creative Play Zone	painting	20
	cooking	10
Imaginative Play Zone	splashing	2
	molding	3
Dramatic Play Zone	role playing	12
Nature Zone	planting	14
Adventure Play Zone	constructing	13
Private Play Zone		
Manipulative Coordination Zone	swinging	22
	balancing	27
	crawling	31
Large Muscle Development Zone	climbing	26
Open Area Play Zone	throw & catching	36

Rules

1 Pick the four (4) most important OBJECTIVES (gold cards) for your playground.

2 Select three (3) ACTIVITIES (orange cards) that satisfy the concept of each objective. Deal with one objective at a time.

3 Place each activity in the appropriate ZONE (brown cards). You may assign any number of activities to any of the zones.

4 Choose one (1) EQUIPMENT SETTING (yellow cards) suitable for each activity.

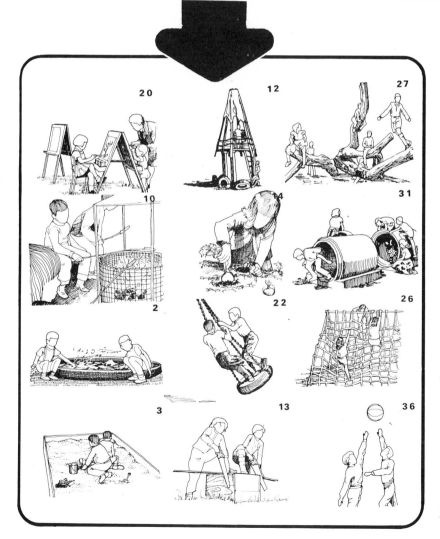

An example of choices made by a parent/teacher group.

pep

playground equipment planning

This procedure can be a useful approach for organizing playground layout ideas. It can aid you in discovering various problems that may arise before you actually build and locate the equipment.

You will however, require the results from Planning Outdoor Play to initiate this procedure. All of the concepts generated by the POP game particularly the use of Equipment Settings and Zones will be applied in this exercise. There are two stages to this process: Preparation and Planning.

PREPARATION

Find a sheet of paper at least 12 inches by 17 inches to draw a ½ inch square grid; or a sheet of graph paper with a ¼ or ½ inch grid already printed. You will also require the use of the Equipment Settings which should be xeroxed and cut along the solid lines. The drawings were made to scale to fit the ½ inch grid which corresponds to four feet.

Measure the length and width of your playground and record this information on the grided sheet of paper.

Match the equipment cards to the zones and arrange them on the graph sheet.

When moving equipment around on the graph sheet, four things need to be remembered:
1.) There is a top and a bottom to each drawing on the cards provided. Keep the direction of all your equipment standard.
2.) Always keep the edges of your equipment cards aligned to the grid.
3.) You can turn the equipment cards over, to reverse their direction.
4.) If you want to decrease the distance between pieces of equipment, feel free to overlap cards.

For example, here's a layout scheme for an adventure play zone.

Once you have an arrangement that you feel is satisfactory, use the Guidelines Checklist provided to evaluate your layout scheme.

Next, tape the graph sheet to the table top in the following manner:

PLANNING

Divide the playground site into the zones you have chosen from the P.O.P. game zones list:

- PRIVATE PLAY ZONE- children use small protected areas for individual or quiet activities.
- DRAMATIC PLAY ZONE- children exercise their imagination to create roles.
- ADVENTURE PLAY ZONE- children spontaneously build and rebuild their environment.
- MANIPULATIVE COORDINATION ZONE- children develop coordination skills frequently with repetitive motion.
- OPEN AREA PLAY ZONE- children use large spaces for group games and individual activities that may require hard or soft surfaces.
- CREATIVE PLAY ZONE- children combine materials to make a different object.
- LARGE MUSCLE DEVELOPMENT ZONE- children overcome physical and mental obstacles, exercising all possible muscles.
- NATURE ZONE- children interact with natural objects.
- IMAGINATIVE PLAY ZONE- children exercise imagination and limited muscular effort, but no may be produced.

Decide what equipment need be placed in each zone before estimating its size. Then, locate your zones to capitalize on characteristics unique to your site-e.g.-shaded areas, existing surfacing, slopes, trees,etc.

If you are satisfied that your arrangement meets the checklist guidelines, place a sheet of tracing paper over the graph sheet and cards, tape it down, then trace the site plus equipment.

(HINT: Use a fine tip felt pen to outline the final tracing for presentation).

You should try several different zone and equipment arrangements, following the same procedure each time, until you have several tracings to compare.

Your committee should then choose one of the tracings as the final plan to show to the entire group at the next general meeting.

See pages 64 and 65 for Equipment Cards.

considered
not considered
not appropriate

☐ ☐ ☐

If there are swings, allow space for moving in front and behind without children getting hit.

☐ ☐ ☐

If there are good, sturdy trees and suitable grassy hills, try to include them in your design plan as play places.

☐ ☐ ☐

If there are tall structures, use soft surfaces underneath in case of falls (Refer to the section about surfaces and safety).

☐ ☐ ☐

Be sure to include places for litter and for small toy storage, and for storing wheeled toys. It is better to have several small closely spaced play areas than one or two large zones.

☐ ☐ ☐

If you have riding toys (trikes, wagons, etc.) leave an open smooth surface where it will not interfere with other activities. The same is true for ball playing - leave enough room for bouncing, throwing and rolling away from windows, streets, or places where the ball may interfere with other children playing in sand, etc.

considered
not considered
not appropriate

☐ ☐ ☐

If you need garden space - put it in a well protected area. Planted areas need borders for added protection.

☐ ☐ ☐

If there are slides, make sure there are at least 4 feet of space around the base, for waiting a turn or just running.

☐ ☐ ☐

Younger children should have separate play areas for safety, but they do not need to be completely separated from older children's play areas.

☐ ☐ ☐

If children of different ages and sizes will be using the playground, make certain that you have allowed for the differences in skill levels. Each age group should have a place where they feel comfortable and play safely.

☐ ☐ ☐

The most popular playgrounds have variety and are located in pleasant areas (sunny in some places, shady in others). Children prefer playgrounds that have familiar types of equipment (swings, slides, jungle gyms); but it also good to have a space for adventure play where they can build their own structures out of tires and light weight boards.

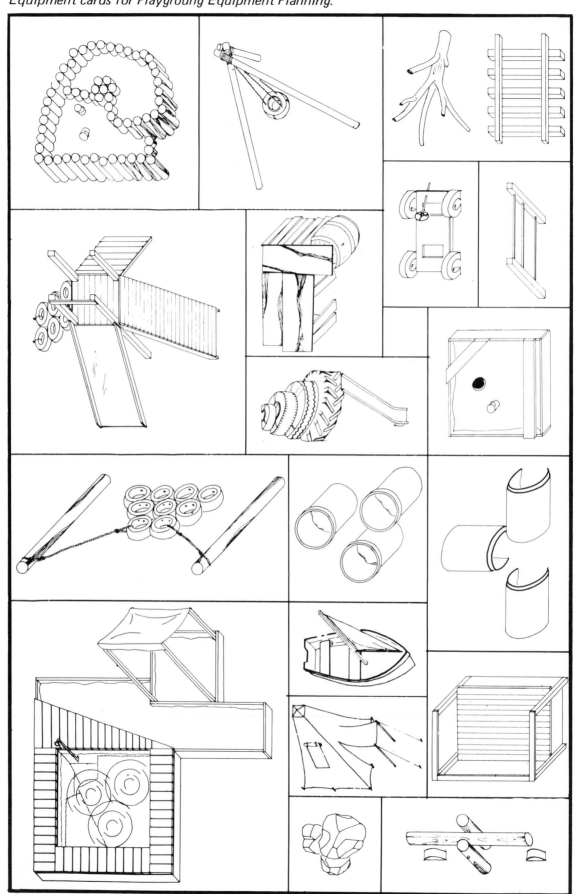

Scaled drawings of playground equipment to be arranged on a sheet of graph paper representing the playground site. Scale 1 inch: 8 feet.

CUT EQUIPMENT CARDS

Use these extra pages to cut out your design aids for playground planning.

Equipment cards for Playground Equipment Planning.

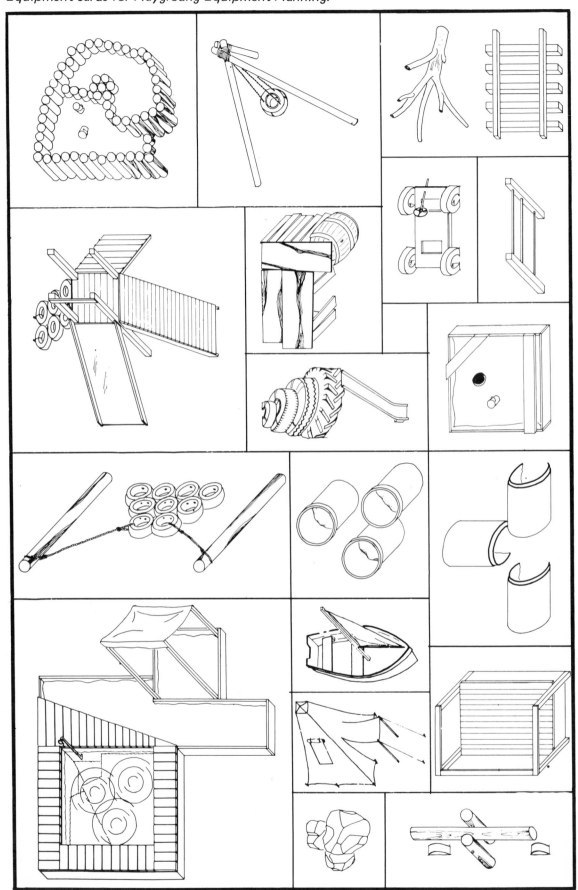

Scaled drawings of playground equipment to be arranged on a sheet of graph paper representing the playground site. Scale 1 inch: 8 feet.

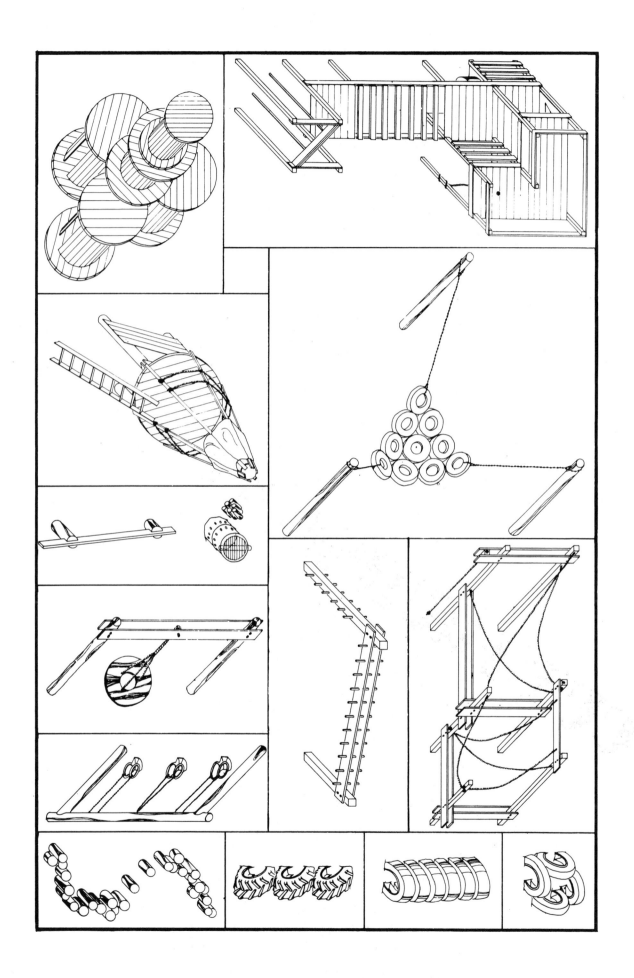

65

CUT EQUIPMENT CARDS

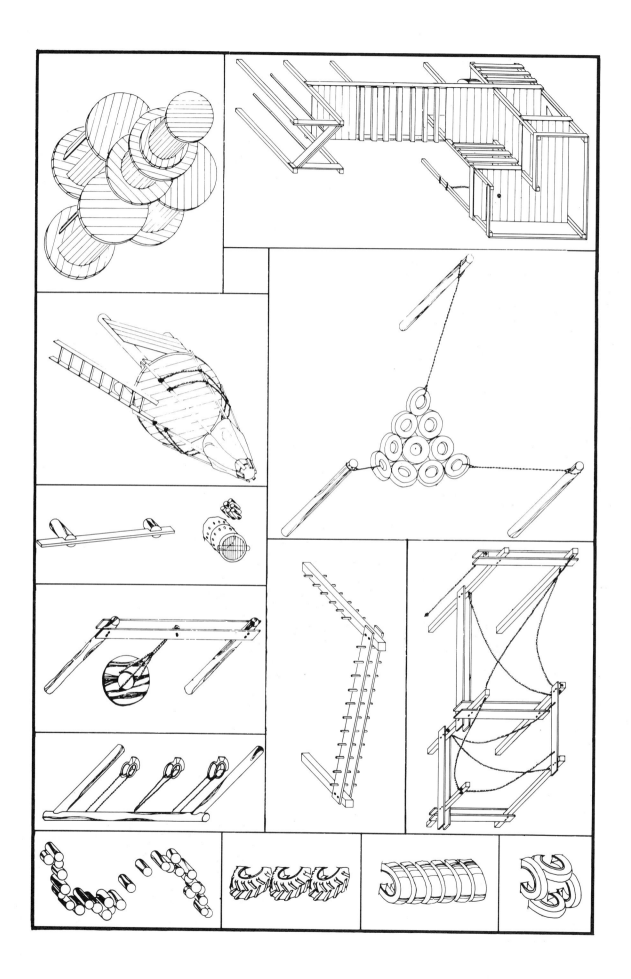

In planning for the effective achievement of your educational OBJECTIVES it is necessary to consider the following:

THE ACTIVITIES YOU WISH TO USE TO ACCOMPLISH THESE OBJECTIVES AS WELL AS THE TYPE OF PHYSICAL SETTING YOU CAN USE TO ACCOMMODATE THESE ACTIVITIES'

The game is planned for groups of three to five people. To begin, each player individually selects, from the list provided, no more than five OBJECTIVES which seem to be of most importance. Brief notes should be made justifying each choice. After each player has made his or her choices, the individual lists are pooled.

OBJECTIVES should be arranged so that they can be seen by all players. (Note: It may be advisable to retype each ACTIVITY and OBJECTIVE on individual cards to facilitate handling the materials with a group.) Through negotiation the group must choose from all the statements no more than five OBJECTIVES that can be incorporated into a unified educational program. Players are urged to forcefully support their individual choices, even if other members of the group did not make the same choices. Continue discussions until consensus is reached on the five OBJECTIVES your group believes to be the most important. This may require considerable discussion which can however be limited to twenty minutes if you desire. After completing this phase, group members should record their final choices on the record sheet.

Next, examine each OBJECTIVE individually and select three or four ACTIVITIES that can be used to accomplish each OBJECTIVE. (You should work through each OBJECTIVE completely before starting a new one.) Keep in mind that some ACTIVITIES may relate to more than one OBJECTIVE.

Then, combining these two elements, OBJECTIVES and ACTIVITIES, choose a physical SETTING that can be used to fulfill the requirements of each OBJECTIVE. Remember, SETTINGS should provide the appropriate props, materials and equipment to allow for the successful performance of the ACTIVITIES on your record sheet.

learning ENVIRONMENTS for children

activities

Art Activities
Manipulatives
Water Play
Measuring
Construction
Animal Care
Cubbies
Table Games
Role Playing
Plant Care
Weighing
Listening
Looking through Books
Music
Block Play
Eating or Snacking
Outdoor Active Play
Cooking
Science Activities
Large Group Games
Sand Play
Resting
Quiet Activities

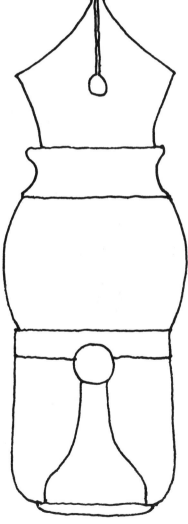

objectives

Developing Language Fluency
Encouraging Student's Sense of Community Identity
Reinforcing Sense of Effectiveness of the Individual
Developing Cognitive Skills
Developing Motivation for Learning
Encouraging Self-Expression
Reinforcing Positive Self-Image
Developing a Sense of Confidence
Developing Persistence Toward A Goal
Developing Concentration
Developing Self-Regulation
Learning by Discrimination
Developing Communication Skills
Developing Concept Formation
Channeling Basic Biological Drives Constructively
Developing/Encouraging Resourcefulness
Developing Initiative and Spontaneity
Developing Introspective Skills
Developing Social Competence
Developing Tolerance of Differences
Developing A Sense of Responsibility
Learning by Conditioning
Encouraging Group Interaction
Learning Through Execution
Stimulating Curiosity and Imagination
Developing A Sense of Reality
Achieving Intra-Sensory Integration
Developing Motor Skills
Learning by Example
Developing Memory Skills
Developing Self-Actualization
Encouraging A Sense of Trust
Constructive Use of Fantasy
Developing Perceptual Acuity
Involving Parents In The Educational Experience
Developing Social Awareness

Activity settings for a early learning children's center.

DESIGN A CHILDREN'S CENTER

Planning the children's center is often a difficult task requiring the knowledge of the Architect as well as that of the early childhood teacher. The problem is similar to that of a child's puzzle. There are a number of pieces that must fit together in some logical manner. Unlike a puzzle, however, there is not only one correct solution or best fit of pieces. The differences stem from the needs, values and goals of teachers, parents and communities. Yet the common aspect to all groups is the kind of activities children engage in and the things they enjoy doing and learn from. The pieces of this game represent what is common to all centers. How they go together or what pieces are included may vary from player to player. This game can provide the preliminary step in planning for physical changes.

Each of the diagrams represents an activity in a children's center. From the set of diagrams it is possible to plan a children's center or a classroom as well as remodel an existing building. The activity diagrams include the administrative services of a center (entry, director, staff, etc.), the children's indoor activities (block, art, manipulative, etc.), and the children's outdoor activities (climbing, swinging, etc.). Through the use of the diagrams it is possible to plan relationships between activities or which activities should be close to one another and which require some separation.

Draw a grid board to correspond with the size of the activity symbols. The rules for the diagrams and the grid board are as follows:

1. Each activity diagram should be placed on a vacant grid.
2. Diagrams should not overlap nor occupy more than one grid cell.
3. Activities should be located on the basis of their requirements for privacy or accessibility to each other.

While many of the activities seem to be related each activity can have direct contact with a maximum of four other activities. This means that the placement of activities on the grid will require a decision on which are the most important relationships.

After going through this planning process, whether you are an architect, teacher, administrator or student, you gain a better understanding of the problems of planning as well as programming for physical changes.

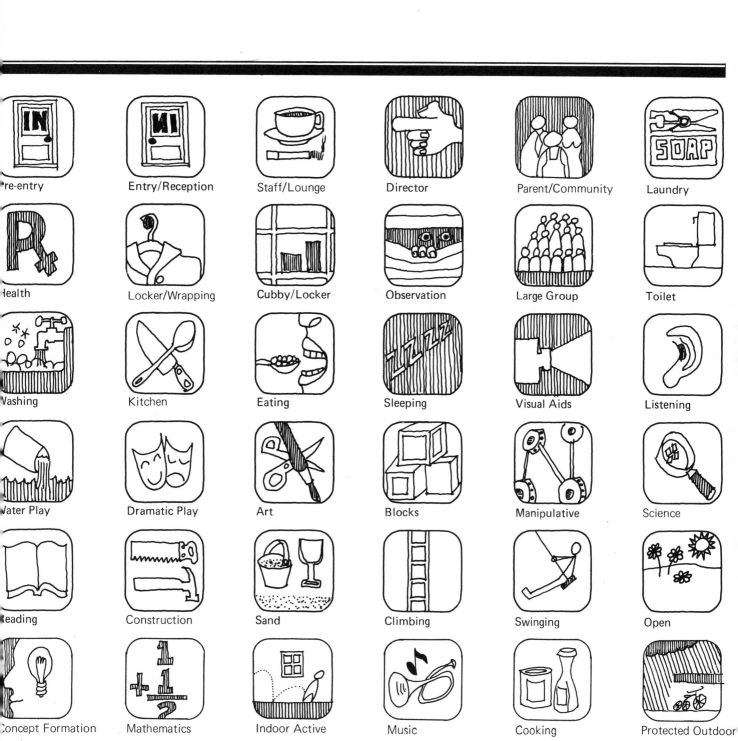

Pre-entry	Entry/Reception	Staff/Lounge	Director	Parent/Community	Laundry
Health	Locker/Wrapping	Cubby/Locker	Observation	Large Group	Toilet
Washing	Kitchen	Eating	Sleeping	Visual Aids	Listening
Water Play	Dramatic Play	Art	Blocks	Manipulative	Science
Reading	Construction	Sand	Climbing	Swinging	Open
Concept Formation	Mathematics	Indoor Active	Music	Cooking	Protected Outdoor

Graphic symbols representing activities in a children's center.

An illustration of activity area relationships utilizing graphic symbols.

Picnic Area	Cinema	Entry	Post Office	Laundry
Shuffle Board	Parking	Music Listening	Ping Pong	Art/Handicrafts
Dining	Reading	TV Watching	Group Meeting	Drug Store
Showers	Reception	Theater	Swimming	Clothing Store
Meetings	Coat Storage	Dancing	Personal Care	Library
Pool	Meditation	Registration	Physical Therapy	Auditorium
Nurses Dressing	General Medicine	Mental Therapy	Dentist	Administration

ON SENIOR CENTER DESIGN

The symbols illustrated on this page were used to represent activity areas in a senior center. Each symbol was selected from an inventory of source books. This abstract notation system is a convenient way to study spatial relationships. Use the procedures described in designing a children's center to experiment with the requirements of a seniors' center.

RELATING OBJECTIVES for LEARNING to EDUCATION

In planning for efficient and effective achievement of educational OBJECTIVES, it is necessary to consider the following:

> LEARNING METHODS to be used to accomplish the OBJECTIVES.
> ROLE RELATIONSHIPS, between student and teacher, whether child or teacher directed. The difference is primarily who makes the decision about the learning activity.
> SETTINGS or environments in which LEARNING METHODS will be accomplished.

NOTE: You may want to make individual game cards for each item on the list as well as xerox and cut the settings into cards. The use of cards is a convenient way to manipulate each item so they can be viewed by the group.

The game is planned to be played by a group of 3-5 people. To begin, each player individually selects, from the listing inside the sheet, no more than 4 OBJECTIVES which seem to him to be the most important. Brief notes should be made justifying each choice. After each player has made his choices the individual lists are pooled, and the corresponding OBJECTIVE cards are pulled from the deck. OBJECTIVE cards are arranged, face up, so that they can be seen by all players. Through negotiation the group must choose from these no more than 4 cards, with the additional constraint that these 4 must be able to be incorporated into a single, unified educational program. Players are urged to forcefully support their individual choices, even if other members did not make the same choice, until they persuade or are persuaded by others that an OBJECTIVE should or should not be included in the final four. This may require considerable discussion. Time should be limited to about 20-30 minutes. When consensus is reached, the group should record its choices.

Use the GAME RECORD sheet to report each of your choices. Next as a group examine each OBJECTIVE individually and select LEARNING METHOD cards which identify strategies for accomplishing each OBJECTIVE. (You should work through each OBJECTIVE completely before starting the next one.) Some METHODS may relate to more than one OBJECTIVE. Choose at least one but not more than 4 METHODS for each OBJECTIVE. The next step is to qualify each of the LEARNING METHODS, whether teacher directed (TD) or child directed (CD) that will accommodate the original OBJECTIVE.

Combining these two elements—OBJECTIVES and LEARNING METHODS—you should choose a physical SETTING conducive to fulfilling the requirements for each OBJECTIVE which will best accommodate your intentions.

methods

Competition
Parent-Teacher-Student Integration
Group Problem-Solving
Student Participation
Self-Presentation
Field Trips
Small Group Discussion
Voucher System
Direct Experience
Role Play/Simulation
Nongraded Classes
Parent Participation
Lecture/Demonstration
Graded Grouping
Remedial Workshops
Self-Directed Activities
Independent Study
Evaluation and Testing Of Students
Open Classroom
Programmed Instruction
Individualized Instruction
Paraprofessionals
Community Resources
Community Involvement
Peer Counseling
Contract Teaching
Team Teaching
Audio-Visual Aids

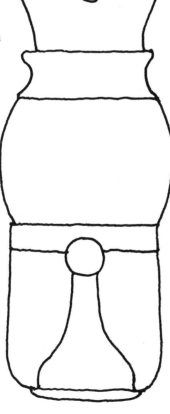

objectives

Developing Language Fluency
Encouraging Student's Sense of Community Identity
Reinforcing Sense of Effectiveness of the Individual
Developing Cognitive Skills
Developing Motivation for Learning
Encouraging Self-Expression
Reinforcing Positive Self-Image
Developing a Sense of Confidence
Developing Persistence Toward A Goal
Developing Concentration
Developing Self-Regulation
Learning by Discrimination
Developing Communication Skills
Developing Concept Formation
Channeling Basic Biological Drives Constructively
Developing/Encouraging Resourcefulness
Developing Initiative and Spontaneity
Developing Introspective Skills
Developing Social Competence
Developing Tolerance of Differences
Developing A Sense of Responsibility
Learning by Conditioning
Encouraging Group Interaction
Learning Through Execution
Stimulating Curiosity and Imagination
Developing A Sense of Reality
Achieving Intra-Sensory Integration
Developing Motor Skills
Learning by Example
Developing Memory Skills
Developing Self-Actualization
Encouraging A Sense of Trust
Constructive Use of Fantasy
Developing Perceptual Acuity
Involving Parents In The Educational Experience
Developing Social Awareness

RECORD SHEET

objectives methods settings

1

2

3

4

See pages 102–105 for enlarged versions of
the ROLE setting photographs at right.

Settings

THE CHALLENGE OF THE ENVIRONMENT

Today many people talk about the problem of the threatened environment. But concern alone is not adequate, and too few people are doing enough to greatly improve the air we breathe, the water we drink or the beauty of our surroundings. "What can I do," you ask, "to become part of the solution?" One way to begin is to decide to live "ecologically" and adopt a life style based on more restrained consumption. Another way is to take individual and group action against polluters. If you become an active friend of the planet earth, you can help set off a chain reaction that might help save the world's vanishing resources and improve the environment.

This is a game originally designed to facilitate the selection of children's camp activities by identifying important environmental objectives and then deciding upon the most suitable location for all the activities selected. It was originally designed for the Pines of Carolina Girl Scout Council in planning the activities of their camp, which is used as an example here. The same methods, however, can be adapted to your community's needs by substituting a map of a local summer camp, a city park or a school recreation area.

environmental objectives

DEVELOPING MOTOR SKILLS

DEVELOPING CAMPING SKILLS

DEVELOPING SELF EXPRESSION

DEVELOP MEMORY SKILLS

ENCOURAGE INITIATIVE AND SPONTANIETY

DEVELOPING PRESERVATION AWARENESS

DEVELOP INTROSPECTIVE SKILLS

DEVELOP A TOLERANCE OF DIFFERENCES

DEVELOP LANGUAGE FLUENCY

DEVELOPING A SENSE OF CONFIDENCE

DEVELOP SOCIAL COMPETENCE

DEVELOPING MOTIVATION FOR LEARNING

DEVELOPING COMMUNITY AWARENESS

DEVELOPING SELF REGULATION

DEVELOPING SAFETY SKILLS

ENCOURAGING RESOURCEFULNESS

DEVELOPING COMMUNICATION SKILLS

DEVELOPING CONCENTRATION

DEVELOPING PERSISTENCE TOWARD A GOAL

DEVELOP ENVIRONMENTAL AWARENESS

Check the topics that interest you and add your own ideas.

rules

The game is planned to be played by a group of 3-5 people. To begin, each player individually selects, from the list provided, no more than 5 OBJECTIVES which seem to be the most important. After each player has made his or her choices, the individual lists are pooled.

OBJECTIVES are arranged, face up, so that they can be seen by all players. Through negotiation the group must choose from these no more than 5 with the additional constraint that these 5 must be able to be incorporated into an environmental program. Players are urged to forcefully support their individual choices, even if other members of the group did not make the same choices. Continue negotiating until consensus is reached on the 5 OBJECTIVES your group feel most important.

Next, as a group examine each OBJECTIVE individually and select 4 ACTIVITIES which can be used to accomplish each OBJECTIVE. (You should work through each OBJECTIVE completely before starting a new one.) Keep in mind that some ACTIVITIES may relate to more than one OBJECTIVE.

Then, combining these two elements- OBJECTIVES and ACTIVITIES- choose a physical SETTING which can be used to fulfill the requirements of each OBJECTIVE. Remember, SETTINGS should provide an environment which allows for the successful performance of the ACTIVITIES.

Pines of Carolina Girl Scout Council

activities

 LODGING
 TRAIL SHELTER
 GROUP CAMPING
 HOSTEL PIONEER CABIN
 CAMPGROUND

 RANGER STATION
 PICNIC SHELTER
 COUNCIL RING
 PICNIC AREA
 CAMPFIRES

 PLAYGROUND
 LOOKOUT TOWER
 TRAILER SITES
 STABLE
 AUDITORIUM

 BATH and SHOWER
 DAM
 WASHING FACILITY
 WATER SPORTS AREA

 SLEEPING SHELTER
 NATURE TRAIL
 SELF GUIDING NATURE TRAIL
 BICYCLE TRAIL
 HIKING TRAIL

 PING PONG
 FISHING
 FISH HATCHERY
 ROW BOATING
 DIVING

 SCUBA DIVING
 WATER SKIING
 BOATING (Sail)
 SHUFFLEBOARD
 POOL (Billiards)

 HORSE TRAIL
 SOFTBALL
 TENNIS
 ARCHERY
 FOOTBALL

 AMPHITHEATER
 THEATER
 GOLF
 SHOOTING RANGE
 WINTER SPORTS AREA

 DEER AREA
 ART
 BASEBALL
 FORDING PLACE
 DOCK

conceptual site plan setting

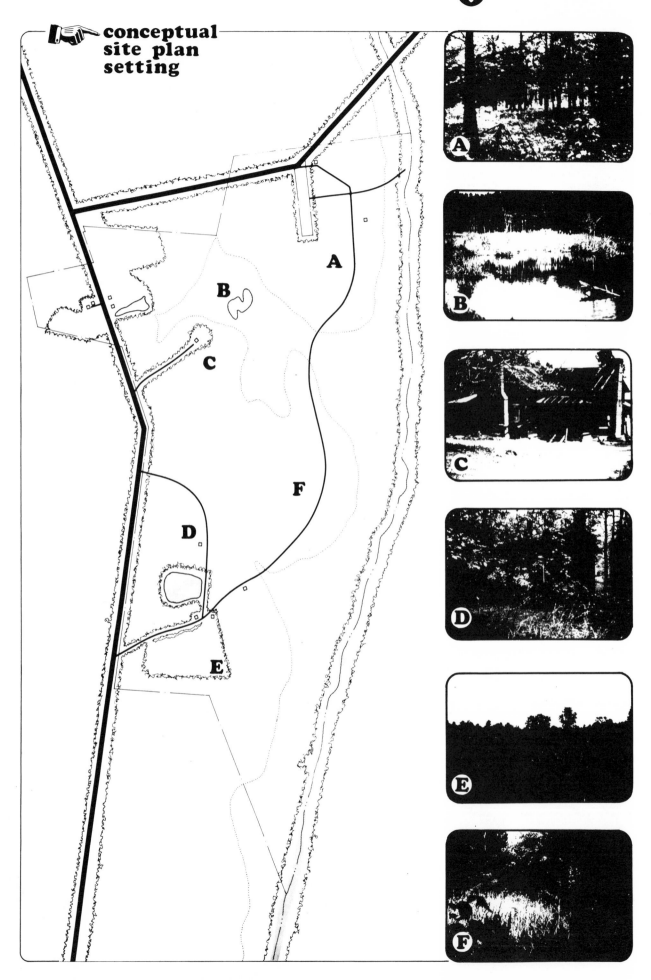

environmental objectives

DEVELOPING CAMPING SKILLS

DEVELOPING SAFETY SKILLS

DEVELOPING A SENSE OF CONFIDENCE

DEVELOP ENVIRONMENTAL AWARENESS

DEVELOPING PRESERVATION AWARENESS

DEVELOP A TOLERANCE OF DIFFERENCES

ENCOURAGING RESOURCEFULNESS

developmental strategy

Nature trails — A-E F
nature trail-self guiding for individual troops

activities

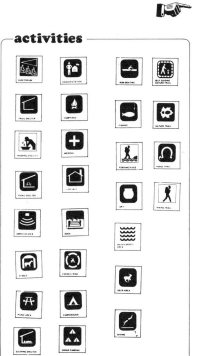

conceptual site plan

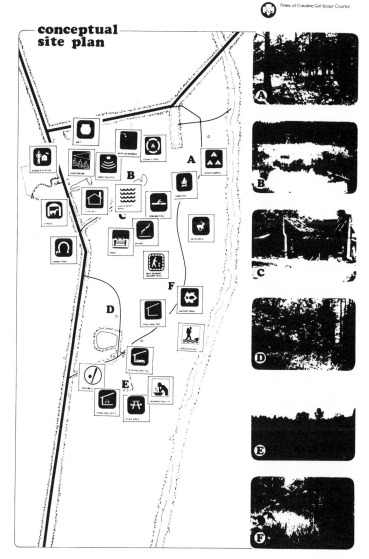

ROLE PLAY

The purpose of this problem solving game is to develop a program for your school so that the architect can create an appropriate environment for learning to occur. A program is a statement about the educational goals and the conditions necessary for them to be achieved.

This role playing game begins with a group of students acting out the parts of the members of a building committee, school board or whatever suits your situation best.

You will need to include all of your "base" information such as the number of students in the school, their ages and whatever information you feel to be pertinent.

Each student can then assume a different decision making role--which will probably be in conflict with each other. It is important to remember to act out each role consistently and have the entire group reach some periodic agreement.

DEVELOP A PROGRAM FOR YOUR SCHOOL PLAY A ROLE GAME

from Henry Sanoff, Seeing the Environment: An Advocacy Approach, (Learning Environments, 1973)

Parent No. 1: You are sending your child to this school so he can be with children of his social level. The public schools expose your child to children you would not want him to become involved with—"children not of his own kind".

Parent No. 2: You feel that this school can offer your child better academic opportunities. You are interested in your child learning the three R's and getting good grades so that he can succeed in life.

Parent No. 3: You feel that the public schools don't understand your child. He does not get along with the teachers. They pick on him for things he does not do and accuse him wrongly. You feel that in this school with small classes and better teachers, he will be better understood and do well.

Headmaster: You, the headmaster, feel that education is self-directed. Each child pursues his own interests at his own rate of development. Each child receives individual instruction as required.

The Architect: You are designing a school for this community. In order to successfully achieve this end, you must find out from the building committee, parents, teachers and headmaster, what the educational objectives are. Each of the participants' contributing ideas may create conflict. Your role is to direct the group to reach some agreement about goals and objectives.

Building Committee Member—Builder: You, as the builder, are concerned with the cost of construction. To you, a good school means sound brick construction at a low cost. You will support most ideas about education as long as they do not interfere with a sound building.

Building Committee Member—Minister: You, the minister, are concerned with religious education. You desire that more time be committed to the teaching of the Bible as an important part of the educational objectives.

Building Committee Member—Doctor: You, the doctor, feel that academic achievement is of utmost importance. There should be an emphasis on learning facts and information and do away with all this freedom nonsense of the child pursuing his own interests. Learn and get good grades so your child can get into a good college.

Teacher No. 1: You believe in a strict schedule: All children do all activities together. They are assigned tasks and must fulfill their assignments. One afternoon a week is set aside for "free time".

Teacher No. 2: You believe that with appropriate materials and guidance in their use, children can proceed at their own rate and interest. They are free to question the teacher and ask for help when needed. Children can move about freely with the teacher's permission.

An illustration of a role playing scenario based on the problem of designing a new school.
You can use roles based on your own design questions and community make-up.

The Community Development Group (CDG) of the North Carolina State University School of Des
used the KEEPS procedure in helping develop preservation strategies for Murfreesboro, North Caroli
These pages show part of their research and planning. The completed project is presented in DESIGN
ING WITH COMMUNITY PARTICIPATION by Henry Sanoff, published by Dowden, Hutchinson a
Ross, Inc., 1978.

MURFREESBORO, N.C.
plan alternatives for
the national register historic distri

In recent years, the small town of Murfreesboro,
N. C. has, under the direction of the local historic association, rehabilitated and adaptively used
several of its old, historically significant buildings. As a result, the community has not only
benefited by the addition of space which has the
potential to support a variety of activities, but
also retains its important educational and cultur-
al resources as reminders of the town's physical
social and economic development. This concept
of conservation through adaptive use is being applied in many places throughout the country and
is widely recognized as a logical approach for
gaining useable space while saving old buildings,
particularly in small towns such as this one.

The first project to renovate and use an historic
building in Murfreesboro began in the late Sixties.
About the same time, a 12-block historic district
was established near the center of town, and control over its development given to the Historic
District Commission and the Murfreesboro Historical Association (MHA). Since then the MHA
has sponsored two other public reuse projects,
encouraged private individuals to restore six old
homes for residential use, purchased several sites
within the historic district for possible reloca-
tion of endangered buildings, and received Federal and State assistance for these and other projects. What was lacking, however, was a compre-
hensive plan to guide future growth for the historic district. Decisions to take action on an
issue was more or less made as resources became
available or as a crisis arose.

The Community Development Group (CDG)
was asked to devise a plan that would enable the
MHA to more effectively make decisions and
direct the future of the historic district. CDG
is a graduate architecture studio at the School
of Design, North Carolina State University.

CENTRAL SECTION~ HISTORIC DISTRICT

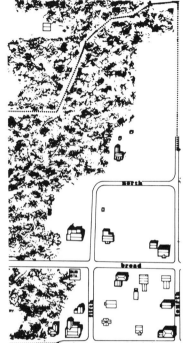

goals related to area

👉 ADD & DELETE AS THE GENERAL GOALS OF THE MHA CHANGE

* Preserve architecturally and historically important buildings

* Boost the community interest and civic pride

* Control change in the historic district

* Use river and ravines to full potential

* Restore many homes to period authenticity

* Involve more people in the MHA's plans

* Improve business along Main St.

* Eliminate the non-historic homes from the historic district

👉 _____

_____
_____
_____
_____
_____
_____
_____
_____
_____
_____

qualities/importance of area

👉 ADD & DELETE AS THE QUALITIES OF THE AREA CHANGE

* Highest density of historic buildings in Murfreesboro.

* Largest concentration of Federal style architecture.

* Oldest buildings in Murfreesboro.

* Rural character still evident.

Area north of Wheeler house

* Rural-town interface.

* Wide range of architectural styles represented.

* Largest concentration of MHA-owned land.

* Borders on largest ravine.

* Part of original town as laid out by William H. Murfree in 1787.

* Largest concentration of historic brick structures in Murfreesboro.

* Thompson house yard includes a large amount of open space, suitable for a wide range of uses.

A group decision making process where alternative solutions are generated from goals

---

* Many architecturally significant buildings.

Wheeler house

* Distinct residential character.

* One block from the CBD.

* Tourist attraction.

* Very little vehicular traffic through or bounding this area.

* Offers room for relocating buildings from elsewhere in town.

* Bounded by a lively residential area.

* One block from the City Hall and community center.

* Close to the Meherrin River.

* Large number of trees and shrubs.

Rear facade of Myrick house

* Includes an old cemetery.

* Large yard space per building.

* The significant buildings express the life styles of the early 1800's.

👉 _____

_____
_____
_____
_____
_____
_____
_____
_____
_____
_____
_____
_____
_____
_____

choosing the `right` plan

👉 EVERYTIME IMPLEMENTATION OF ANY GENERAL OR SPECIFIC SUGGESTION IS CONSIDERED UNDER ANY OF THE FOLLOWING ALTERNATIVE PLANS, GO THROUGH PROCEDURE FOR CHOOSING THE 'RIGHT' PLAN IN THE PREVIOUS CHAPTER

implementing the `right` plan

👉 IF THE MHA HAS DIFFERENT, BETTER, OR MORE EXACT SUGGESTIONS FOR IMPLEMENTING ANY OF THE FOLLOWING ALTERNATIVE PLANS, GO THROUGH THE DESIGN GUIDELINES IN THE FOLLOWING CHAPTER TO DETERMINE IF THE SUGGESTIONS ARE ACCEPTABLE

alternative plan 1

👉 SCRATCH OUT ALL SUGGESTIONS THAT ARE NO LONGER PERTINENT OR HAVE ALREADY BEEN IMPLEMENTED

policy
A program promoting a distinct historic image for the area should be implemented.

effect
Area will have the largest density of significant structures in Murfreesboro

general suggestions for implementation

* Existing MHA funds should be used to rehabilitate/restore MHA-owned buildings presently located in the area, rather than for moving buildings into the area from other locations. Follow the priority list below for spending on rehabilitation/restoration of MHA-owned buildings in the area:
  (1) restore the Ferguson house exterior [1]
  (2) rehabilitate exterior of the building on the SW corner of Broad St. and Fourth St. [1]
  (3) restore the Thompson house exterior [1]
  (4) restore the exterior of the Winborne Law Office [1]
  (5) rehabilitate interior and restore exterior of Peter Williams house [1]
  (6) restore the interior of the Winborne Law Office [1]
  (7) rehabilitate interior of the building on the SW corner of Broad St. and Fourth St. [1]
  (8) restore exterior of Murfree Law Office [2]
  (9) rehabilitate the interior of the Thompson house [2]

keeps

Knowledge of Emerging

Environmental Preservation Strategies

KEEPS is a game designed to provide groups, interested in preserving the many environmental **qualities** unique to older neighborhoods, districts and towns, with an understanding of the **strategies** open to them. Organizing and planning for the preservation of the **qualities** your group has identified as important, relies upon the consideration of:

The environmental **qualities** your group seeks to develop.

Your **goals**.

The type of **strategies** your group can realistically use to accomplish your **goals**.

To begin, each player selects from the **goal** list provided, no more than four **goals** that seem to be important in developing the environmental **qualities** your group has decided upon. When making your initial selections, brief notes should be made justifying each choice. When all the members of your group have made their **goal** choices, the individual lists are pooled.

Through negotiation the group must choose a total of four **goals**, with the additional constraint that the four statements must be incorporated into a unified conservation program. Players are urged to forcefully support their individual choices, even if other members of the group differ. Discussion should continue until group members persuade or are persuaded to include four **goals** that reflect the groups priorities. This may require considerable discussion.

When consensus is reached the group should enter its choices on the record sheet.

Next, using the **strategies** list, each player should individually select no more than four implementation **strategies** that can be used to effictively accomplish each of the **goal** choices. Work through each **goal** completely before starting a new one. And, keep in mind that some **strategies** may relate to more than one of your **goal** choices. After all members of your group have made their **strategy** selections, pool your lists and negotiate on your final group selections. As before, players are urged to persuade the total group to include their own particular selections.

Your completed record sheet now contains the framework of a collaboratively generated conservation program. Combine the results of all the working groups and use these as a framework for future discussions and actions. Remember, the future is up to you.....and KEEPS is what we are playing for.

GOALS

Preserve historically significant sites, landmarks. objects, and buildings.

More public and private involvement in decisions which could alter the character of the area.

Heightened public awareness of the area's unique physical character.

Optimal use, or re-use of sites in the area.

Preservation of the neighborhood's visual characteristics.

Influence public and private investment for the good of the area.

Neighborhood development which is compatable with the long range objectives for town development.

Public awareness of the area's historic resources.

Preservation of neighborhood social cohesiveness.

Maintenance and upgrading of properties.

Increased public participation in the development of the area.

Influence neighborhood improvement programs in other parts of town.

Control of growth and development in the area.

STRATEGIES

Encourage property owners to increase property maintenence.

Encourage civic organizations to clean up, or maintain sites.

Offer preliminary architectural services to businesses and individuals interested in developing sites.

Encourage private planting programs.

Move some historically significant building into fill a key unoccupied site.

Encourage pedestrian activities in key areas by petitioning for walkway improvement programs.

Contact other organizations that have initiated similar projects for advice.

Have an area wide 'planting day'.

Develop detailed design guidelines to maintain a consistent area image.

Organize for bulk purchase of materials.

Acquire public agency support.

Encourage the demolition of buildings that are hopelessly beyond repair.

Use local media sources to obtain issue visibility.

Look into the possibility of federal and state grants.

Lobby for zoning changes which can insure the implementation of your goals.

Purchase and restore key buildings and sites to 'period authenticity'.

Sponsor continuing area wide 'clean up day' programs.

Identify and evaluate historically significant buildings and sites.

Purchase, rehabilitate, and adaptively re-use significant buildings and sites.

Develop property easement programs and standards.

Put utilities underground.

Purchase, rehabilitate and sell.

Purchase, rehabilitate and rent.

Control   outdoor advertising.

Develop a revolving fund.

Tree planting and maintenance of publicly   owned property.

The cartoon above is a story about changes that have occured through the years in an imaginary town (not unlike your own). Organize into groups of three to five players. Then, as a group, discuss and list on your record sheet the qualities and characteristics that were lost through the process of change. Try to be as specific as possible; include only those qualities that your group agrees upon.

ENVIRONMENTAL QUALITIES:

RECORD SHEET

1

2

3

4

from Henry Sanoff, *Methods of Architectural Programming,* (Dowden, Hutchinson & Ross, 1977)

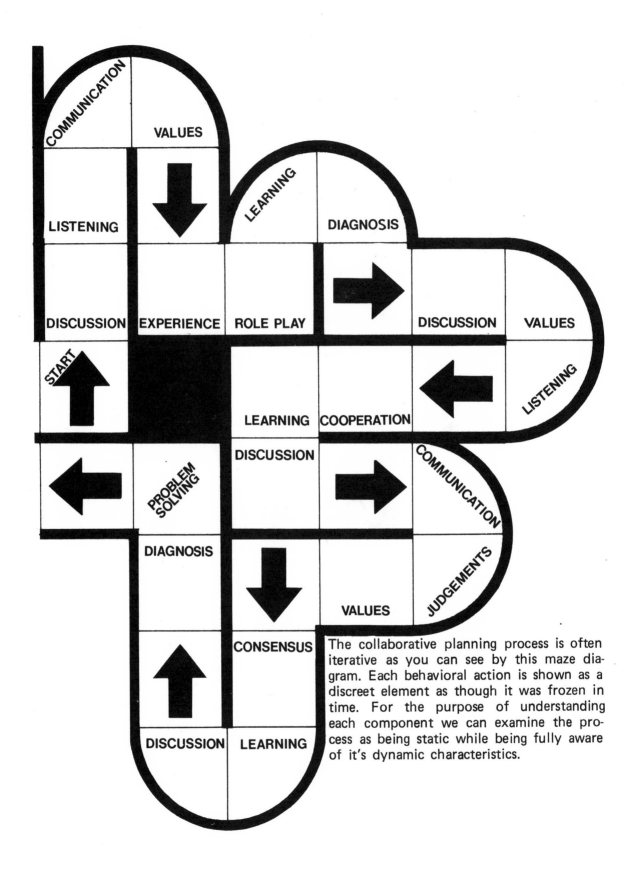

The collaborative planning process is often iterative as you can see by this maze diagram. Each behavioral action is shown as a discreet element as though it was frozen in time. For the purpose of understanding each component we can examine the process as being static while being fully aware of it's dynamic characteristics.

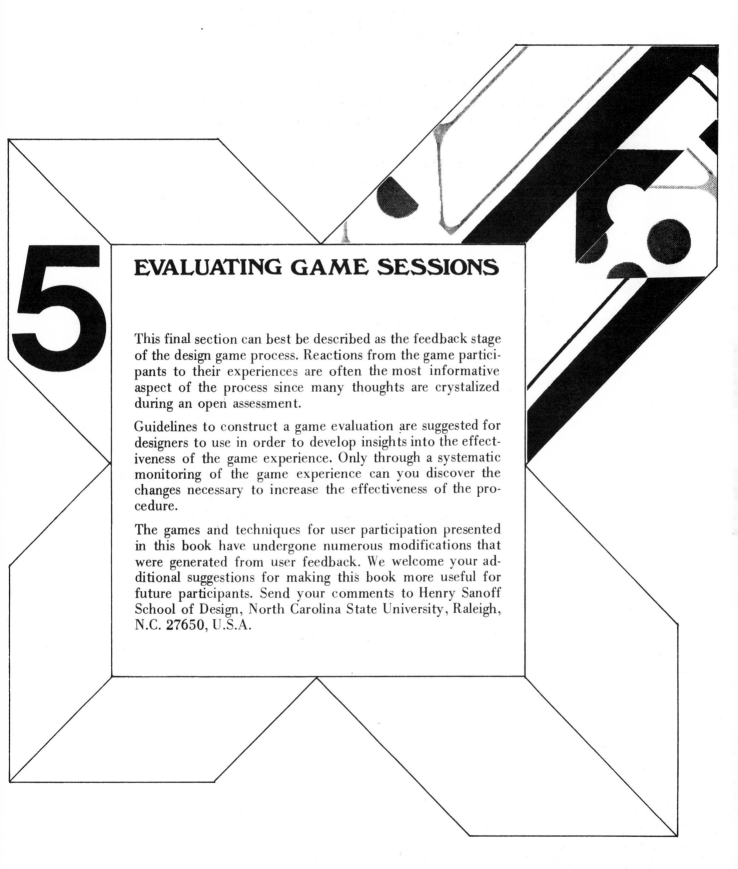

5

EVALUATING GAME SESSIONS

This final section can best be described as the feedback stage of the design game process. Reactions from the game participants to their experiences are often the most informative aspect of the process since many thoughts are crystalized during an open assessment.

Guidelines to construct a game evaluation are suggested for designers to use in order to develop insights into the effectiveness of the game experience. Only through a systematic monitoring of the game experience can you discover the changes necessary to increase the effectiveness of the procedure.

The games and techniques for user participation presented in this book have undergone numerous modifications that were generated from user feedback. We welcome your additional suggestions for making this book more useful for future participants. Send your comments to Henry Sanoff School of Design, North Carolina State University, Raleigh, N.C. 27650, U.S.A.

The results of a game experience are important to the game designer as well as to the players. Assessments can be made about the game session as well as the validity of the game model.

For such an assessment, a final discussion among players is an important part of the game process. Sometimes the most important learning occurs at the end when some conscious effort is made to convert the experience into some knowledge or insight. We evaluate primarily to determine whether the goals and objectives of the game operator were met. Where learning is involved there can be many different goals and the success of the game session is in the appropriateness of the game to the particular objective.

A useful approach to evaluation can be to understand what happened from the viewpoint of all the participants and compare those views to the goals of the game operator. To help answer the question, "What went on here?", you can use these questionnaires or one of your own devising.

questionnaire

1. Please check the statement below that best describes your feeling about this session.
   A. Excellent   B. Interesting   C. All right   D. Mediocre   E. Uninteresting

2. What are the strong points about the process?

3. What were the weaknesses?

4. Did you find new concepts that will be useful to you? (Circle one number)

   0.   1.   2.   3.   4.   5.   6.   7.   8.   9.   10.
   none   many

5. Were the materials used during the session helpful?

6. Were the methods used for group participation effective?

7. Do you feel that you will be able to implement ideas gained through this experience?

   0.   1.   2.   3.   4.   5.   6.   7.   8.   9.   10.
   none   many

8. What improvements would you suggest for future applications?

questionnaire

Occurred	Did not occur	Most important	Least important	
				LEARNING THROUGH ROLE PLAY
				1. Gaining skill in that particular role and improved ability to perform in a real situation.
				2. Learning to negotiate and communicate.
				3. Understanding the dynamics of the system to which the role belongs.
				4. Opportunity to experiment with strategies designed to change the social and political structure.
				5. Developing greater empathy for that role.
				6. Experience in applying and testing knowledge gained from reading and other experiences.
				LEARNING ABOUT DECISION MAKING
				1. Acquiring critical thinking, analytic and decision making skills.
				2. Learning the importance of establishing policies and making long range plans.
				3. Discovering constraints and contingencies that are not usually considered.
				4. Encouraging systematic analysis of the rewards of alternative strategies.
				5. Getting used to making decisions and learning to use interpersonal aspects as in real decision-making.
				6. Learning to act within certain constraints in the system.
				7. Learning how to grapple with the problem of urbanization.
				LEARNING ABOUT HUMAN BEHAVIOR
				1. Learning how to communicate better with others who have different perspectives.
				2. Identifying goals, objectives and value structures in your own and others behavior.
				3. Developing a feeling for the need of communication.
				4. Learning about interaction among different subgroups.
				HAVING FUN
				1. Finding it pleasurable to participate in a group.
				2. Breaking the ice.
				3. Having fun in the process of play.
				4. Enjoying the complexity of the games.
				5. Having a valuable although not necessarily an exciting session.
				TECHNICAL ASPECTS OF THE SESSION
				1. Game operator enhances understanding.
				2. Time of day was right.
				3. Pace of game added rather than detracted.
				4. Time spent playing games was sufficient.
				5. Game equipment made the game easier to follow and more realistic.
				6. The critique session clarified and reinforced the game experience.

Players' response — Occurred / Did not occur

Operator's objectives — Most important / Least important

Abt, C., *Serious Games,* New York: Viking Press, 1970.

Boocock, S.S. and Schild, E.O., *Simulation Games and Learning,* Beverly Hills, California: Sage Publications, 1968.

de Leon, P., "Scenario Designs: An Overview", *Simulation and Games,* Vol. VI, No. 1, March 1975, p.39-60.

Duke, R., *Gaming Simulations in Urban Research,* Institute for Community Development and Services: Michigan State University, 1964.

Halprin, L. and Burns, J., *Taking Part: A Workshop Approach to Collective Creativity,* Cambridge, Massachusetts: MIT Press, 1974.

Hanks, K., Belliston, L. and Edwards, D., *Design Yourself,* Los Altos, California: William Kaufmann, 1977.

Harrison, R., "Self-Directed Learning: A Radical Approach to Educational Design", *Simulation and Games,* Vol. VIII, No. 1, March 1977, p.73-94.

Jackson, S., *A Gamut of Games,* New York: Random House, 1969.

Koberg, D., and Bagnall, J., *The Universal Traveler,* Los Altos, California: William Kaufmann, 1974.

Liggett, H., "An Evaluation Instrument for Use with Urban Simulation Games", *Simulation and Games,* Vol. VIII, No. 2, June 1977.

Meier, R., "Game Procedures in the Simulation of Cities", *The Urban Condition,* New York: Basic Books, 1963.

Orbach, E., "Some Theoretical Considerations in the Evaluation of Instructional Simulation Games", *Simulation and Games,* Vol. VIII, No. 3, September, 1977. p.341-360.

Sanoff, H., *Seeing the Environment: An Advocacy Approach,* Raleigh, N.C.: Learning Environments, 1973.

Sanoff, H., *Methods of Architectural Programming,* Stroudsburg, Pennsylvania: Dowden, Hutchinson and Ross, 1977.

Sanoff, H., *Designing with Community Participation,* Stroudsburg, Pennsylvania: Dowden, Hutchinson and Ross, 1978.

A

SPACES THAT CONNECT

C

E

G

SPACES THAT CONNECT

I

J

K

L

SPACES THAT CONNECT

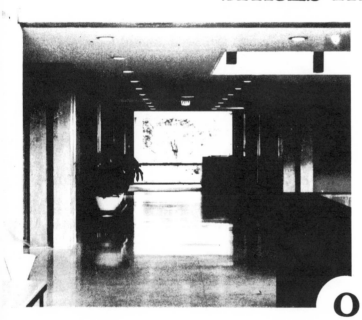

S

T

SPACES THAT CONNECT

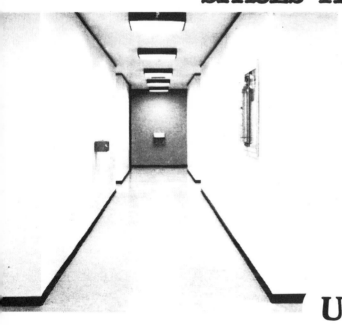

U

V

W

X

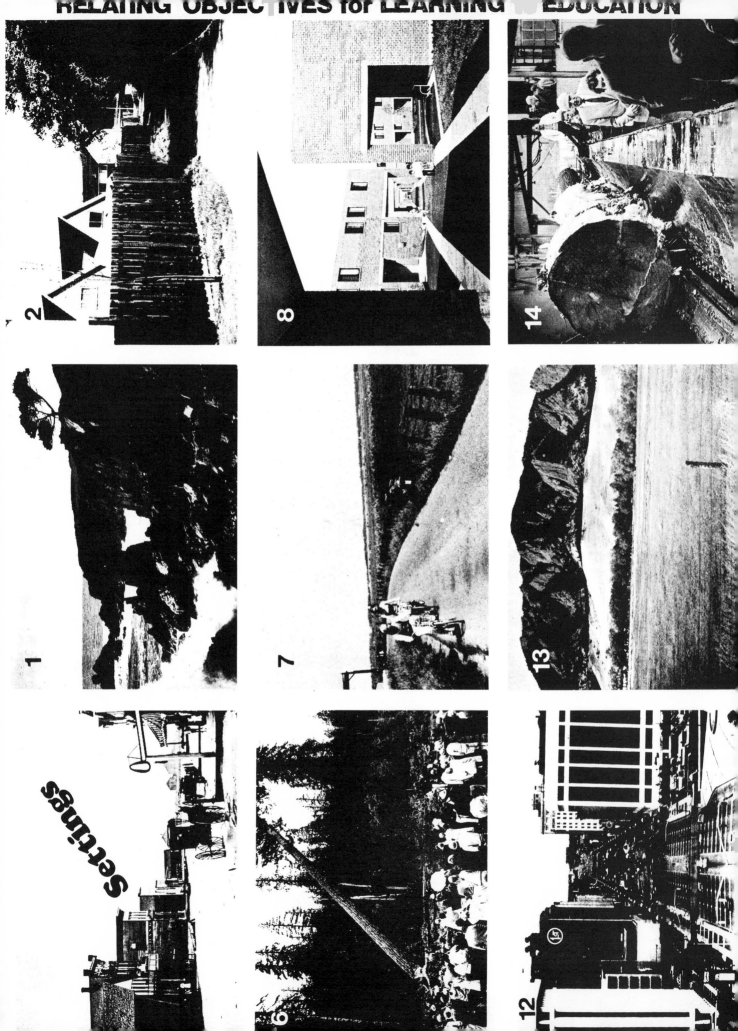

Settings

2

8

14

1

7

13

6

12

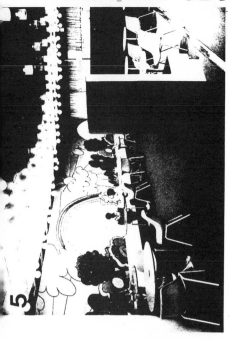

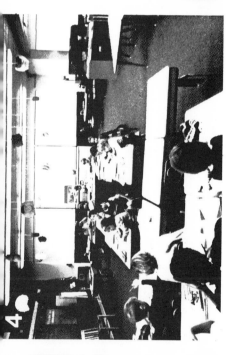

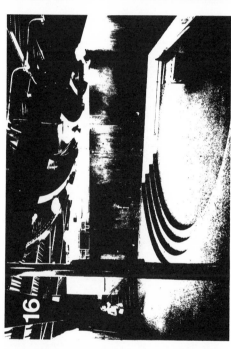

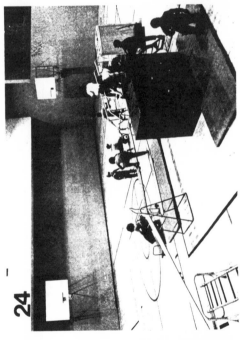

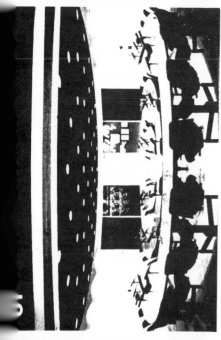

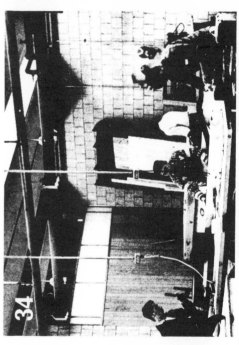

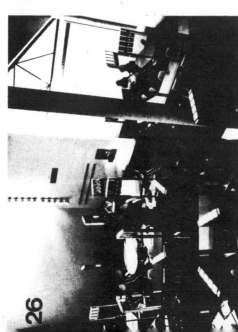